Live Your Best Life

Live Your Best Life

How to Go From Surviving to Thriving After Abuse

Selene Bartolo

All Rights Reserved. No portion of this book may be reproduced, stored in a retrieval system, or transmitted in any form or by any means-electronic, mechanical, photocopy, recording, scanning, or other-except for brief quotation in critical reviews or articles, without the prior permission of the publisher.

Published by Game Changer Publishing

ISBN: 9798656987394

www.PublishABestSellingBook.com

This book is dedicated to my little girl
whose voice was silenced for so long
and all the children around the world who
have been abused, hurt and silenced for life.

DOWNLOAD YOUR FREE GIFTS

Read This First

Just to say thanks for buying and reading my book, I would like to give you a free bonus gift that will add value and that you will appreciate, 100% FREE, no strings attached!

To Download Now, Visit:

http://www.SeleneLifeCoach.com/SB/freegift

Disclaimer

This program is intended as educational material only. Nothing in this book should be construed as psychological or medical advice. Always consult a professional when needed. The author of this book disclaims any liability in connection with the instruction, information or advice given.

Live Your Best Life

How to Go From Surviving to Thriving After Abuse

Selene Bartolo

www.PublishABestSellingBook.com

Table of Contents

Introduction 1

Chapter 1: Are You A Victim Or Not? 5

Chapter 2: How Abuse Affects You 16

Chapter 3: How Addictions Help To Cope After Abuse 25

Chapter 4: Why You Attract Energy Vampires 36

Chapter 5: Is There Any Hope For A Happy Life? 51

Chapter 6: Free Yourself From Trauma Bonding 64

Chapter 7: You Are The Most Important Person 79

Chapter 8: Finding Your Power, Your Voice And Speaking Your Truth 96

Chapter 9: Exiting Toxic Relationships 104

Chapter 10: Finding Freedom, Peace And Love 115

Chapter 11: Living Your Best Life 125

References 138

Introduction

People walk around with pain in their hearts, unable to reach their full potential. Other people are trapped in abusive relationships without an end in sight, never able to break the cycle. I remember the feeling in the middle of my storm. It felt like I was pushing through a snow blizzard on a very cold windy night out in the wilderness. The wind and cold snow freezing my face and body, I could not even lift my head because the blizzard was so strong. I remember thinking, "Where am I going? How do I get out of this mess?" Having no clue which direction to go and no one to guide me, I just kept pushing forward. I forced my legs to push forward one step at a time. I held on to a slight hint of hope that somehow, someway, I would make it out alive. The abusive cycle never stops or changes for the better on its own. You have to break it. I have experienced abuse since I was a very young child. The abuse continued my entire life extending from one relationship to another. I was not able to break free from the cycles but instead kept repeating them over and over without understanding why it continued to happen. I told myself I would NEVER accept abuse. I always heard stories where the victim goes back for more. I set in my heart that would never be me. However, when I look back, I experienced all forms of abuse: physical, psychological, spiritual, financial, emotional and more. I did what I could to help myself. I tried therapy, counseling, praying, journaling, joining support groups, etc. Nothing helped me to stop the cycle or be abuse free. I felt trapped and unable to stop it or help myself. I allowed these things to happen to me. But why? I didn't know why. I knew I deserved better. I knew I should not allow these things to happen to me or allow other people to treat me that way. However, I could not prevent or stop it from continuing to happen. I felt guilty and full of shame to ask for help or expose what was happening to me, which kept me stuck. Even though my life moved forward, I didn't enjoy it. I was miserable no matter what I did or accomplished. I kept going through the motions of life because I knew I had to. I went to college, worked hard and took care of others. Despite the abuse, I became an overachiever, trying to win everyone's love and admiration. I thought this was the way to be loved and accepted. I became the provider and focused on others. Other people's needs, wants and problems became my responsibility to fix or fulfill. I did very little for myself or the things that made me happy. As a full time student, working more than 65 hours a week in a highly stressful job, newly wed with six step children, I finished my undergraduate and masters degrees in business. I also had extreme success in my career, I was Vice President of a mortgage branch, financial center, credit & underwriting department. I owned nice homes and luxury cars. I was physically fit and attractive. I had a seemingly perfect family and a respectable job earning good income. Unfortunately, I found those things did not bring me joy, happiness or peace. My life was crumbling around me. Then the bottom fell out and I didn't know why this was happening to me again. Why couldn't I make it work? The big WHY. I was a good person and I followed all the rules. I was a lawful citizen, a servant of God and my community. In order to find out the reason, I went on an educational and spiritual journey to figure out why.

I quickly realized I was focusing on all the external factors. I was trying to control the people, places and things in my life in order to avoid feeling pain. I discovered I could not control others. I could not change people, places or things. The only person I had control over was myself, my thoughts, feelings and reactions. I learned to focus on myself. I had to find myself where I was and be open to change. The definition of insanity is doing the same things over and over again expecting different results. All I knew was that I did not want to keep repeating the same cycle over and over again. It wasn't until I found a life coach and mentor, Bird Mejia, who helped open my eyes. I started to piece everything together in my life. The things I had learned all came to the forefront and I was able to pull the thread that tied it all together. I was able to take off on my healing journey to find peace, happiness and joy. It is a journey that never ends. Friends and family tell me I'm a different person today who now radiates from the inside. I found my strength and courage to face my pain in order to heal it. I found myself and followed my life, passion and dreams to help others do the same.

CHAPTER 1

Are you a victim or not?

For our purposes, a victim is a person who is deceived or cheated, as by his or her own emotions or ignorance, by the dishonesty of others or by some impersonal agency. There are many types of victims and survivors. This book was written for survivors and/or current victims of abuse. If you are a survivor of abuse, you may be wondering if your past abuse affects your present life. Or perhaps you may not realize how much your past does affect your current and future life. I didn't think my past affected me at all. There are many types of abuse, some we don't even know about or think are abusive, especially if you grew up surrounded by it. The following types of abuse can happen alone or in conjunction with one another, which is more often the case.

- There is physical abuse which is easy to identify visually through bruises, cuts, burns, or specific behavior
- Verbal abuse includes derogatory comments aimed at minimizing and breaking a person down emotionally
- Sexual abuse, including forced sex (even if married), rape, unsolicited derogatory sexual comments, aggravated assault, selling victim for sex and more
- Mental abuse is similar to emotional abuse but it differs in that a person's mind is made to feel unreliable while second

guessing of self. It's almost like making a person feel they are crazy using gas lighting

- Spiritual abuse, less commonly known, when someone uses God or religion as a way of manipulating someone by making them feel guilty, unloved or unaccepted if the person does not behave a certain way or comply with their demands. As I grew up, I always felt guilty and unloved by God. I felt as if I deserved everything bad that happened to me because I was a bad person

- Financial abuse involves manipulation for the sole purpose of gaining money or things of value or even a certain lifestyle from the victim. The abuser may guilt the person into buying them clothes, paying their bills or other "urgent things." It can also include taking them out to eat, buying expensive items like cars, jewelry or taking them on vacations. The red flag is buying things for the perpetrator not necessarily out of need or a one time event. Another red flag is when the victim hands over life savings for a business venture in which he or she never receives a return or profit. The money given is for the profit of other people putting themselves in last place, especially when it doesn't benefit him or her. The abuser may even manipulate the person to upgrade the home or household items to the point of bankruptcy; when the person can no longer afford to keep up with the lifestyle.

- Intellectual abuse, where a person is used for their intelligence to get something of value like money, a lifestyle, or advancement in the world of business. A victim may be used for their ideas and the abuser takes the credit

- Psychological abuse involves power imbalance, not limited to bullying, gas lighting or abuse in the workplace

- Ambient abuse is changing the environment to create minor noticeable changes and then denying it in order to cause distress to the victim. They want the victim to believe they are imagining it. This type of abuse is tied closely to gas lighting where false information is presented to the victim to make them doubt their own perception or memory to question their own sanity

- Coercive control is a form of abuse that uses several methods aimed at intimidating, isolating and controlling the victim. The forms of abuse include: indirect abuse, intimate terrorism, or emotional torture

- Economic abuse is where the victim's resources are limited or diminished. Ensuring the victim can not leave the abusive relationship because of lack of money. The abuser takes over the finances and gives the victim a meager allowance even if the victim is the one working. The abuser may also destroy the victim's property and blame him or her for the inability to support themselves.

There are many obvious types of abuse that are recognizable from afar. The ones that are not so obvious are the most dangerous because there are no warning signs or red flags for those inside the cycle of abuse. Usually, this is the norm for someone who grew up in this type of environment. Growing up, I was told that God didn't love me if I didn't behave properly. So I grew up thinking that if I did anything wrong, then something bad would happen to me. When

I started my period, I didn't know what it was. I literally thought I was dying. I thought God was punishing me because I wasn't obeying the rules or the laws I was taught from my parents, the teachers and the church. I was so scared and ashamed I didn't tell anyone. I was just waiting to die. I was so fearful, until the nurse at school explained what was happening to my body. My mother later explained she didn't think it was time to tell me because I was so young. Using God to manipulate behavior is a form of spiritual abuse.

There are so many types of abuse to varying degrees. Most of these tactics are used to manipulate the victim to act to the abuser's advantage and believe in them as the utmost authority. The perpetrator asserts their power and control by abusing the victim. All of these types of abuse aim at making the victim do things or believe things about themselves that are not true. Being in a false sense of self, victims fear leaving because they believe they will suffer more outside the relationship.

As a young girl, I endured tremendous abuse, starting with physical, verbal, sexual and psychological abuse. The earliest memory or recollection I have was when I was 3 years old; although I think it started earlier than that. I remember being very angry and raging inside. I was threatened to be killed or my mother killed if I said anything. I remained quiet and suppressed all the feelings of rage and hate inside. Eventually, as I grew up, these feelings turned into self-hate because I blamed myself for everything that happened to me. As if it was my fault or that I deserved it. These beliefs about myself impacted the rest of my life in profound and severe ways. As I continued to live my life from these beliefs, I made decisions and choices that did not benefit me. These choices based on false-beliefs, cost me a lot in terms of the quality of life I lived. I will discuss these choices and decisions throughout the book as I lived my life with a lot of triggers.

Triggers

You may be wondering what I mean by triggers, what they are and how to identify them. Triggers are intense feelings that do not match a situation you're in. So, for example, it's reasonable to be afraid of the dark, but instead in a trigger you feel terrified. It's reasonable to be lonely, but instead, a triggered person feels abandoned. A triggered person often tends to think in black and white, in extreme absolutes and from irrational thoughts. These feelings are very overwhelming and extremely difficult to work through. A triggered person can feel desperate, panicky, attention seeking, needy, and/or fantasize about solutions that aren't possible. These are all examples of how you may feel when you're triggered. What is really happening to you is you just went back in time to when you were a child trying to manage adult problems. The event that caused the trigger, mirrors a time when as a child you felt the same way. The feelings could be those moments when you felt trapped, abandoned, neglected, ignored, powerless, frightened, and unable to change the circumstance. The thoughts are considered flashbacks. They come in short spurts, but the emotions involved can be overwhelming. The memories are brought to the forefront in certain situations which can cause you to act out as a child in those moments. For example, being outside in a certain part of town where you grew up. It could be a certain time of the year like birthdays or holidays. Depending on when the trauma occurred, time of year, certain smells, doors slamming or pictures can be big triggers for people. Hearing certain voices or pitches, if somebody is yelling at you, may also create a trigger as well. A simple smell of food or grass, can cause a trigger and memories start to flow. The triggers take a person back to the roots of when, where, and how it started. These roots from childhood are still unresolved, unsettled, and unexpressed feelings. The child may have felt enmeshed with family members. Enmeshment is a psychological term that describes a blurring of boundaries between people, typically family members. It often contributes to dysfunction in families and may lead to a lack of autonomy and independence that can become problematic. In this dysfunctional environment, emotional wounds like toxic shame and false beliefs about the inner identity can be created in a young child. The triggers can last minutes, weeks, months or even years. They can also lead to spirals.

Characteristics of Enmeshed Families

©2019 Sharon Martin, LCSW

- Lack boundaries
- Children not encouraged to individuate and become emotionally independent
- Intrusive or needy quality to relationships
- Over-sharing or demands to know all about your life
- You're expected to conform to family norms and traditions
- Self-expression is stifled
- Parents may treat children as friends or confidants
- It's not acceptable to have opinions, beliefs, or ideas that differ from the family's
- Fierce loyalty is expected
- Guilt and shame are used to maintain the status quo

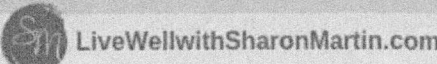
LiveWellwithSharonMartin.com

Spirals

You may ask, what I mean by spirals. Spirals are what happens when a triggered individual can not come back from the irrational thoughts to the rational side. It is the inability to bring self back to wholeness and peace. When triggers lead to spirals, the person is going from one irrational thought to another, creating a story about the people, places or things in their lives that is based on false data, beliefs and/or perceptions. The person may start acting on those irrational thoughts and triggers, creating even more trauma and pain. The spiral continues to feed the false beliefs and it goes on and on. While someone is spiraling out of control, the person continues to act out in their child like state. He or she may react impulsively, immaturely or even aggressively. What is happening here is that the person goes into survival mode. This is the instinct side of the brain that shifts into gear, designed to help us escape life or death threats. It bypasses the rational side of the brain so our body can take over and get us out of danger quickly before we get seriously injured. This is also known as fight or flight mode. What happens biologically in the body is dilation of your pupils, dry mouth, fast breathing, heart pounding, muscles tense up and hands sweat. The amygdala sends signals to the hypothalamus to release adrenaline and the adrenal cortex to release cortisol for continued alertness.

Coping Skills

You may be wondering how someone copes when they find themselves in a trigger or a spiral. First, you want to stop what you're doing. Whatever it is, stop and just take a deep breath for several minutes, while closing your eyes. Try this three point breath: breath in slowly for 4 seconds, hold for 4 seconds and release slowly counting down 4 seconds. With each exhale imagine the anxiety exiting the body. You can sit or lie down in a comfortable position. It also helps to take a piece of paper and start journaling whatever comes to mind. Close your eyes and feel where the trigger is located in your body or in your memory. Start journaling and writing whatever comes to mind without any judgment, let it flow. Go back to your little child, back to the trauma or whatever comes to your mind to really let it out by writing it on paper. Understand where it's coming from in order to process and release it. It's important to understand what caused the trigger. Stop and ask yourself, what am I feeling? What am I afraid of? What am I angry about? Where is the pain coming from? What is shame telling me? Really spend time until you narrow down exactly what triggered you. When did it start? How did it start? What were you doing? What was said to you? Think back; was it a smell, a sound, a TV show or a movie that triggered you? Try to pinpoint when exactly you started to feel triggered. Go back and try to identify a previous memory where you had the same experience and listen to your body. Be really open and understand what is triggering you. It is important not to run away from these emotions in order to heal them. Allow whatever comes to mind and don't excuse or brush anything off. Whatever comes up could be what caused the trigger. It is important to keep in mind, not to make any decisions while you're in this childlike state. Do not make decisions regarding relationships, work, money or moving. I reiterate, do not make major life changes while you're triggered. Remember, the triggers and emotions are about you, not the other person. Wait until you're calm and you feel your normal self again before making these major life decisions. When we're not working from our rational state, we can make major mistakes that can not be reversed. Your decisions are not going to be based on facts. They will be based on emotions that are not grounded on truth. You want to make sure you bring yourself back to balance and back to wholeness. Back to your grown-up state before making these decisions.

It is very important to understand the triggers, why you feel the way you feel. Trace it back to the roots to understand what triggers you and throws you in a spiral. Being able to identify when you're in a spiral will prevent you from making major life mistakes. Sometimes our mind conceals or blocks out trauma that was too much to process as a child. However, it still resides in our subconscious memory. Once you clear out the trauma, you can prevent triggers and spirals linked to it. You want to wait until you are calm and working from your rational state of mind and have clarity. Then and only then can you make the right decisions for yourself.

My first memories of abuse was when I was about three years old. I was watching TV and he called me over. I was very angry and raged that no one could stop the events, not even me. He was violent when I fought back. He threatened to kill my mom and I if I ever said anything. This went on for what seemed forever. It even happened in broad daylight. Once I remember fighting back, he almost suffocated me with a pillow. It made me so angry, I raged inside that I could not protect myself. I carried all of this rage most of my life. I was also angry at my parents for leaving me. I grew up with nightmares of being struck with horror and trying to scream. However, no voice would ever come out, as if my vocal cords were cut out. I had these nightmares throughout my life. I grew up with this deep anger, but I remained quiet and suppressed all the feelings of rage. It eventually turned into hate and then self-hate. I blamed myself for everything as if it was my fault or that I deserved it. These false beliefs about myself impacted the rest of my life as I continued to live in triggered states. I spiraled feeling out of control, making decisions that were not best for me, especially when it came to relationships. I started my life, by making major life decisions about college and where I lived around a cheating lying boyfriend who I later ended up marrying.

CHAPTER 2

How Abuse Affects You

The abuse I endured as a very young child, set the paradigms and subconscious patterns that I lived from for the rest of my life. I created false beliefs like, "I am not lovable" and "My feelings are not worth the trouble to express them." Scientific research by Dr. Bruce Lipton, states that up to the age of six, a child lives in theta state. Theta is a state when automatic download into the subconscious mind occurs and the brain accepts everything that is happening as absolute truth. The child is not in a conscious state and can not reject information. Their brain just accepts everything into the subconscious mind like pressing a record button. The child is a sponge absorbing everything in their surroundings without a filter. This later becomes the programming from which the child bases life decisions, like software. The software coding tells the computer how to interpret the keystrokes and commands from the person using the computer. As such, subconscious programming is how we interpret everything in our world. When a child is in an abusive situation or traumatic event, false self-beliefs become ingrained in the child's inner identity. A lot of times in abuse, the victim takes on the shame and guilt of the abuser. The mind blocks out a lot of pain in order to protect ourselves. However, many of those memories are stored in our subconscious mind and arise later in life. The mind and body want to process, release and heal the pain. We continue to encounter similar people and situations in order to heal.

Your Subconscious Mind

The subconscious mind, what is it? According to Sigmud Freud, the subconscious mind defines all reactions and automatic actions, we can become aware of if we think about them. For example, when we start to learn how to ride a bike, we are aware of every movement in order to balance and get the necessary momentum going and pedaling just right. Once we learn it, we just do it automatically, without thinking about what we are doing. The unconscious mind stores memories we can not remember like when we first learned to walk, we do not remember the feeling or how we took our first steps. In contrast, your conscious mind knows, remembers and processes the day to day activity when you're awake. The subconscious mind processes events during sleep mode through our dreams. During REM, our brain activates the visual cortex, the amygdala (emotional center) and the hippocampus (memories) (Bell 2014) Link. The dreams play out the daily life events to process them during sleep. No one really knows exactly why we dream, but scientists believe it's a way to cope. There is a saying that goes like this, "we are what we eat." I also believe we are what we think. Our thoughts create energy and this energy extends to our body and into our cells. Our cells receive signals from our brain and follow instructions on how to react and respond (Scitable 2014) Link. The programming we received up to age 6 is what created our subconscious patterns. We learned how to interact with our environment, our family and friends. Our caregivers influenced us as children on how to interact with our world. Most of our thoughts are automatic and we replay records we are not aware of. You may catch yourself thinking thoughts that are totally off character or that you do not want to focus on. I know I had a lot of negative self-talk growing up and throughout most of my adulthood. Different types of traumas impact our thoughts, how we process these thoughts and how we interact with the world. As we grew up into adulthood, our subconscious patterns played a big role in how we experienced life. We followed situations, people and places that reminded us of our childhood. In some of these cases we helped create similar situations like trauma-bonding. I will review what it is in chapter 5 in more detail.

However, our subconscious patterns create more of the same patterns that we experienced as children without realizing what is happening. As adults, we are naturally attracted to or feel comfortable with the environment that we grew up in. This is all we ever learned. We gravitate to what feels comfortable to us, even though it may not be what we want. We instinctively gravitate to those environments and people that remind us of our childhood. The environment we grew up in affected our gene expression also known as epigenetics.

Epigenetics

What is epigenetics? In short, it is how our genes express themselves. Genes are a set of instructions that determine what the living being is like, its appearance, how it survives and how it behaves (Medical News Today 2020) Link

We inherited 23 chromosome pairs from each parent that contain our genes or blueprint that make us who we are. Humans have about 20,000 to 25,000 genes! Genes are made from a substance called deoxyribonucleic acid or DNA. DNA is the chemical that appears in strands of genes. Every cell has the same DNA but each person's DNA is different. This is why everyone is unique. The genes are the blueprint that determine our personality, behavior and who we are.

Genes are made up of DNA. Each chromosome contains many genes.

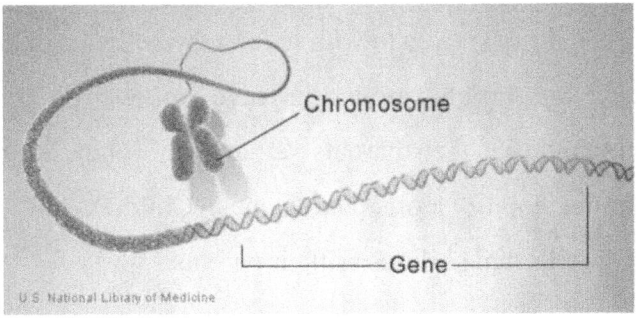

Credit: U.S. National Library of Medicine

Scientists at Harvard University have concluded both nature (what we inherit) and nurture (environment) affect early childhood development (Epigenetics 2019) Link. The genes we inherit are expressed differently based on chemical marks we receive from our environment. It explains why identical twins turn out to be different in behavior, skill, and achievement. Harvard researchers explain: "When experiences during development rearrange the epigenetic marks that govern gene expression, they can change whether and how the genes release the information they carry." This means the environment or nurture, whether positive or negative in early childhood, can determine how the genes are turned on or off, or if they express themselves at all later in life. All of the following impact epigenetics: nutrients in food, how parents interact with children and other people, toxins in food, toxic stress, ambiance, etc. The external and internal environment while a baby is in the womb also affects and changes his or her genes chemically! If the mother while pregnant feels stress and anxiety, guess what? The baby feels it too and so begins the blueprint programming! The opposite is also true, while a baby is spoken to with love in the belly, he or she kicks and reacts to the stimulus around it. Have you ever observed how children mirror what their parents say and do? They even like or dislike similar foods, sports and games. Children have similar athletic or intellectual abilities as their parents.

The environment a child grows in shapes and forms their gene expression. Genes are passed down from the parents and also learned by observation. Does this mean adults are doomed if they come from a toxic environment, absolutely not! However, a reversal of the epigenetic effects has to occur and will require a lot of determination. If we can help young children and young adults deal with these traumas, they can avoid going through the same patterns as their parents. Nothing about this topic is taught in schools or college. If we want to change our future, we need to start with our kids. However, we can not help our kids, if we do not help ourselves first. The latter chapters in this book will show you how you can free yourself from pain and trauma.

The Effects of Long Term Stress

During and after the abuse stress is very much alive and activated. The stress can continue throughout the life span if trauma remains unhealed. A lot of evidence and research exists on how stress negatively affects our immune system. However, long term stress is especially lethal to health. If not handled or managed down to proper levels, it can lead to high blood pressure, heart disease, obesity, diabetes and so much more.

During stress our bodies are in fight or flight mode ready to get us out of trouble. Severe trauma or trauma not dealt with can lead to post-traumatic stress disorder (Shiel 2017) Link. During this disorder, the person may experience severe fear, anxiety, flashbacks, loss of interest, mistrust, loss of pleasure in activities and more. These experiences can lead to depression, illnesses and worst of all suicide. Guilt, loneliness, isolation, nightmares, emotional detachment or unwanted thoughts are prominent in the lives of those who suffer from PTSD.

Living in fight or flight mode has always been part of my life. When I would go to the chiropractor to get an adjustment, he would always say, "Your muscles are so tense, it feels like you were in a car accident." Of course, I wasn't in an accident, I just carried all my stress on my shoulders and back. I was always ready to escape in case something bad happened. I knew where the nearest exit was to get myself out of danger. I always planned for the worse to happen. I remember living in isolation and feeling very lonely. I didn't let people in. I bottled my emotions and feelings. I never talked about what happened or how I was really doing. I always said I was fine even though inside I was feeling pain. We were raised to pretend everything was fine even though it wasn't. As a matter of fact, I believed my childhood did not affect me as an adult. I thought I had a normal and happy childhood. I truly and honestly believed this! I never talked about it, not even with my family. Everytime it came to memory, I rejected the thoughts, never accepting its effects on me or my body. I lived in denial for a very, very long time.

Throughout my life I experienced a lot of nightmares as I stated earlier. I dreamt about being trapped in my home or being back in my old home where I grew up as a child. I was trying to escape or someone was always chasing me. I have dreamt I was dying after being wounded. I also had nightmares where I was held down by this entity that was much stronger than me. Paralized with fear, I couldn't scream or yell even though I tried with all of my heart and soul. I also experienced a lot of detachment from my body (dissociation) and from other people including friends and family. I just didn't know how to reach out to people. I felt very socially inadequate and I felt high anxiety in social settings around other people. I just wanted to live alone and not experience or deal with people in social settings. I basically lived my life in extreme anxiety, low self-esteem, no self love, lots of rage and with a post-traumatic stress disorder. I had so much anger inside of me as a child and a young adult that I would punch holes in walls. I grew up believing that my life didn't matter. I truly believed I was a bad person that deserved everything that happened to me because it was all my fault. My false belief was that I had to be perfect and obey all the rules to even be somewhat worthy of love. I honestly believed my needs and wants didn't matter, like I didn't have a right to them. I also believed the world or someone was out to get me. I never smiled or laughed because I believed that if I did, something bad would happen. I never felt safe to be me. All of these beliefs stemmed from my subconscious mind, I was not aware of them. All I wanted to do was die and disappear from the face of the earth. Those first years of life set the foundation, core beliefs and subconscious patterns for the rest of my life. Especially since those are the most formidable years of life when the brain is still in theta state. In order to deal with these effects, survivors of abuse often tend to fall more easily into addictions.

CHAPTER 3

How Addictions Help to Cope after Abuse

An addiction is a repetitive habit pattern that increases the risk of disease and/or associated personal and social problems, often experienced subjectively as 'loss of control' (Griffiths n.d.) Link. Addictions help to cope but in unhealthy ways. Remember back in chapter one, I talked about how my choices affected the rest of my life in many profound and severe ways? Instead of healing my inner wounds and feeling the pain in order to process through it, I ran away from it. I ran away for fear the pain would be too much to survive. As a result, I lived my life in unhealthy behaviors or addictions. Once we understand addictions are one way to cope, although an unhealthy way to avoid feeling the pain or trauma, we can begin to heal in order to not fall into them again. The thoughts we create in our bodies turn into the energy that fuels our behavior. We are what we think. While avoiding our feelings and emotions, distractions or addictions come into the picture.

Types of Addictions

Many people picture drug usage when the word addiction is used. However, there are many other types of addictions. Some other well known examples are porn, sex, smoking, gambling or alcohol abuse. Have you ever considered these as addictions: food binging or denying, work-a-holic, sports fanatic, over-the-counter medicine abuse, perfectionism, relationships, religiosity, working out, codependency, cutting, gaming, social media, busy work, volunteering and more?

It was an eye opener when I considered these other addictions. Anything we use to avoid our pain in extremity can be considered an addiction. It is a way to avoid dealing with problems or issues. I went from one addiction to another. The one addiction that became my "drug of choice" was to become a work-a-holic. When I wasn't working or in school, I worked out. I spent numerous hours trying to avoid feeling any type of pain. I just dug myself into work and school. I remember leaving in the morning around 6 a.m., going to school, working and coming home around 11:00 p.m. I did not like being with myself or my emotions. When I was younger, on the weekends, I would go out with friends and stay out all night, sleep for a few hours and go to work the next day. By not facing my pain, I didn't heal it and I continued in vicious cycles. As I continued these cycles, I avoided the feelings of shame, guilt, loneliness, anger and rage I felt inside.

As I grew up into a young adult, I used my relationship with my boyfriend as a way to avoid myself. I made everything in my life about him. I focused on him and I built my life around him. I picked a college close to him. I moved out of state to be with him. However, he ended up being exactly like my abuser, although it wasn't obvious to me at first. I trusted him 100% and I gave him so many more opportunities than he deserved. Behind my back, he was cheating and living like a single man. He kept blaming me for his choices. I ended up marrying him only to end in my first divorce, as he continued to lie and cheat on me. He controlled my every move, how I dressed and what I did. I never received love or attention at home, so I clung onto him in order to feel loved. I didn't learn to love and accept myself just the way I was. I always tried to be perfect in order to be loved. I focused on others to make them happy. If they were happy then I was happy. I also used religion and God in my early childhood. It actually helped me from taking my own life at the young age of 10. I had lived with suicidal thoughts up to that point. I didn't want to be in this world continuing to live in the pain I felt. I was miserable because I bottled up my emotions. Even after all of this, I truly believed that nothing impacted me from childhood as an adult since I forgave and forgot. I was not supposed to harbor hate or unforgiveness. I never dealt with the pain and the emotional rage I felt. I felt judgment from people if I said anything. I held false expectations of others. I fell into severe depression and anxiety, it was a constant feeling, unless I prayed but it was only while praying that I felt relief. The feelings of shame, guilt, anger and rage are all feelings that if not dealt with can lead to addictions.

In active addictions, you're just continuing to avoid dealing with the pain. It's a way to cope, but it's not a good way to cope because again, you're not dealing with or healing the inner wounds from childhood or trauma, even if the trauma happened in adulthood. When we don't heal or change the beliefs we created about ourselves in those traumatic situations, then we can't move on past them. We stay stuck in them until we heal those wounds. These addictions are a cover up and a mask. It keeps you from really doing the inner work necessary to remove those thoughts or situations from yourself. What is worse is that you keep repeating the same cycle over and over.

Why we can't break the cycle

Why do we keep repeating the same cycles? We keep repeating the same cycles due to epigenetics, paradigms, trauma-bonds and subconscious beliefs. The abuse cycle is very difficult to break because we are not even aware of the dynamics at play. A lot of the patterns of behavior reside in our subconscious mind. When we were children we accepted everything around us as truth. We did not have the capacity to decipher in order to accept or reject things that happened around us. As adults, we can reject ideas or words that do not agree with us. However, as children what we are exposed to is accepted as our truth. We operate from these paradigms until we change them. A lot of these paradigms or subconscious beliefs are fear and shame based. We actually vibrate these beliefs throughout our body. There is a law of vibration, the law basically states that everything is in motion, even the walls vibrate. It begins with our thoughts that usually originate from our subconscious beliefs. These thoughts or feelings send chemical signals to our body's cells to mirror the same vibration whether positive or negative.

In order to understand how to reach health, wealth and happiness, we must understand the law of attraction. The frequency or vibration in which we feel will attract more of the same. Fear attracts more fear, creating another situation where you feel more fear. Happiness attracts more happiness, you will find yourself surrounded by things and people that make you happy. The law states what you feel or vibrate attracts more of the same. Understanding your vibrations will help understand why you keep going in circles. Good or high vibrations include happiness, joy, peace, calmness, positivity and overall good feelings. Bad or low vibrations include fear, panic, sadness, negativity, anger, hate and more. When you are in a good/high vibration and a bad/low vibration comes into your space, it doesn't feel good. You can feel the turbulence in the energy. However, when we are in a low vibration and someone with a low vibration comes into our circle, it feels good because both vibrate in the same vibration. However, when you change your thoughts, you change your vibrations and you can change your life. Your thoughts create more of the same vibration. As you raise your vibrations, you'll have higher levels of vibrations come into your life. You will start meeting and attracting people with higher vibrations as yourself. However, when you relive your trauma with triggers or if you're stuck in a toxic environment, you keep attracting more and more of the same. You keep repeating the cycle of abuse because you have not healed or freed yourself from those thoughts, vibrations of pain or sadness.

Pain and suffering was ingrained in my subconscious mind since I was a child. I kept creating more of the same. I kept running away from my pain and stayed distracted in unhealthy patterns. When I wasn't working or in school, I volunteered. I volunteered a lot of hours after work. I would stay volunteering until eleven o'clock at night. I stayed busy and I held on to an inner identity of shame and guilt. I didn't love myself. I hated my body, looks and everything about me. My second coping mechanism, which has been the most prominent my entire life was codependency.

What is Codependency?

Codependency is an emotional and behavioral condition that affects an individual's ability to have a healthy, mutually satisfying relationship. Also known as "relationship addiction" because people with codependency often form or maintain relationships that are one-sided, emotionally destructive and/or abusive. In the relationship one person enables another person's addiction, poor mental health, immaturity, irresponsibility or underachievement. This behavior is learned and passed down from generation to generation. It is observed and learned in abusive and dysfunctional families, according to "Codependency." (Mental Health America 2020) Link.

13 Signs You're Codependent
www.lisaaromano.com

1. You feel guilty even though you did nothing wrong.
2. You feel abandoned over the slightest situation.
3. You are overly responsible for the irresponsible.
4. You worry more about what others think about you than what you think about you.
5. You don't trust others could really love you.
6. You are anxious and don't feel good enough.
7. You suffered emotional neglect, abuse, and childhood abandonment and rejection.
8. Your parents were addicts, immature, dysfunctional, abusive, codependent, and or narcissistic.
9. You people please as a way of life.
10. You feel stuck and hate yourself because you don't know how to change.
11. You either cling or push people away.
12. You tend to have turbulent relationships.
13. You stay in toxic situations long after you should and fail to set boundaries.

In my codependency, I focused on other people's thoughts and feelings instead of my own. If everyone else was OK, then I was OK. I based my sense of self on what others thought of me. I tried to earn their love by making them happy instead of myself.

Another way I tried to earn love was by being perfect. I didn't think I was good enough if I was anything less than perfect. In school and work, I had to be the best. I had to be number one. I had high expectations for myself. I did the best I could to be number one and stayed focused on whatever it took to be the best. I believed this is how I could be worthy of love. I also had high expectations of perfectionism in my family. When they didn't act or behave the way I wanted them to, then I raged at them. I made them feel guilty in my disappointment of my expectations. I reflected my own belief of myself onto them as if they weren't good enough. Ever since I was a little girl, I never felt worthy so I wanted those around me to feel the same way.

The knowledge of the importance of understanding our addictions and how to break them is paramount. The way to break the addictions is accomplished by embracing what we're trying to run away from, whether that is pain, trauma or all of the above. By holding them and processing through them, we can begin to remove the painful effects from our lives. We can resolve the issues or false beliefs we hold in our mind. Sitting with them is very difficult and very scary. However, it is worth the work. Once you come out on the other side, you will feel so relieved. You will feel happy, joyous and free.

There are many types of addictions, including surfing social media for hours with no real production. The movie options on Netflix, Prime Video, You Tube, HULU and others all feed the urge to escape reality and immerse in self-avoidance. Using relationships as a means to feel good about oneself, is also another way to avoid pain and afflictions. It's so important to be with yourself, feel your emotions, get toxins out of your body in order to heal. All of the toxins that poison our thoughts create more of the same reality. Who wants to stay stuck in addictions? Who wants to create more of the same trauma? I don't think anyone wants to; however, a small amount of people actually do the work to get out and change their future. The main reason is few people realize the power of the subconscious mind and the paradigm from which we were raised. There is a lack of knowledge. We are not taught how to deal, process and heal our pain or problems at home or at school. We are not taught how to self-love or how to embrace our feelings. We are not taught how to change our way of thinking or how to change our paradigms. I think it's time for change and it starts with you and me. Are you ready for change? What addictions have you suffered from?

Codependency Symptoms

Shame

Denial of needs, feelings, addiction

Perfectionism

Low Self-Esteem

People Pleasing

Guilt

Intimacy Issues

Dependency

Dysfunctional Communication

Painful emotions - Fear-anxiety, depression, despair, hopelessness

Control

    Warped Sense of Responsibility

    Top Dog - Underdog

    Caretaking and Enabling

Dysfunctional boundaries

CHAPTER 4

Why You Attract Energy Vampires

You might be wondering what the heck is an energy vampire? It sounds like a movie theme doesn't it? What is it exactly and what does it have to do with you? When I first heard the term energy vampire, I thought it was some kind of silly joke or imaginary character. However, when a second person pointed it out, I began to understand that they are real people living off the energy of others!!! That is a very scary thought that blew my mind away and it took me a while to actually understand and believe it. An energy vampire is someone whose ego is never satisfied. They are also known as narcissists. There is a range within narcissism ranging from normal to psychopathy. Normal narcissism involves realistic high self-esteem with a balanced emotional state. On the unhealthy side, a narcissist has a serious mental health disorder. Similar to their victims, they had a traumatic event or abuse in his or her early life, probably at the hand of a narcissistic parent. However, they handled it or allowed it to affect them completely differently. They take on the attitude and mentality of their abuser. They avoid their inner wounds to not feel their pain. They do not really like who they are. They create a false self with beliefs of superiority (God like), a sense of entitlement and believe others are there to serve their needs. In order to feed their insatiable ego, they need narcissistic supply in the form of constant attention and admiration. There are many types of narcissistic relationships. Parent to child, sibling to sibling, boss to employee, friend to friend, etc. In this chapter, I will discuss a "romantic" narcissistic relationship. Initially, the narcissists are very charming. They make you believe you are their soul mate and they never met anyone like you. They sweep you off your feet with compliments and even gifts to lure you in. They become what their victims need and want them to be. This is considered the idealization or honeymoon state. Soon after, they become very controlling of your time and whereabouts. They want you home quickly from work to be near them. They start the ambient and coercive control where they make you second guess yourself in the form of gas lighting. You are now in the second phase called the devaluation stage, now you can do nothing right. Their goal is to target the victim's self confidence, self-esteem, and sanity. They try to avoid being alone so they do not face their real inner souls so they need constant attention. They are not capable of feeling empathy, remorse, or feelings of regret. These people never change.

How do you identify them? They are not easy to spot in a social setting. Most of the time, everyone loves them. They are the life of the party because they love attention. They carry on their persona's like great actors. However, they're totally different in private than in public. You will recognize them by their behaviors. At home or in private settings, their actions do not match the words. They deny things they say or do as if it never happened, even when you can prove them wrong. They are master manipulators at using psychological warfare. They undermine their victim's rights by creating ambiguity and uncertainty. Their goal is to cause the target to not trust their own reality and sense of self. They find a way to make you feel awkward or at odds end. They are chronic cheaters as if they are entitled to sleep with as many women or men as they please. They seek the constant energy supply through admiration, attention and sex. One person can not meet all of their demands; therefore, they usually have many victims providing narcissistic supply. When they get caught, they will deny it at first, even if you present evidence. They tell you what you want to hear and make you believe in their lies. Deep down you don't really want to believe how someone could be so callous and disrespect you in such horrific ways. If they acknowledge it, they blame you for the cheating, making you feel guilty for not meeting their expectations or ignoring them. They will continue to cheat until the next time they get caught and the same cycle repeats itself. You have now moved to the discard state. If they feel discovered or if you longer provide the narcissistic supply, they will leave you at the drop of a hat and go to find more narcissistic supply as if they never knew you.

They are great con artists, making you believe they will never cheat on you again. They isolate you and pull you away from friends and family. They twist your words and turn everything on you, as if you are the abuser causing all the problems. In the final stages, they practice hoovering, which happens after they discard you. Even though they have moved on, with or without your knowledge, they still want your energy. They engulf you by constant texting, emailing, calling and sending direct messages. They tell you they love you. They constantly want to know what you are doing, or who you are with and when you are going to see them. When you do see them, after they get sex from you, they give you a huge guilt trip and make it all about them. They make you feel guilty for having a life or wanting to do something for yourself. They accuse you of doing the things they are doing, like cheating and lying. They attack what you love the most: your kids, work, passions, etc. The cycle of abuse repeats and usually gets progressively worse if you do not cut them off.

The abuse cycle starts with the honeymoon phase, the build-up, act-out/abuse, and last rationalize-justify (The Cycle of Abuse n.d.) Link. When people come from a traumatic background or abuse, they are more susceptible to becoming victims of narcissistic abuse. They are especially "easy" targets for energy vampires. These predators can sense the fear, self-doubts and lack of confidence. They use these self-doubts as a way to trap the victim. The victims learned to survive their abuse in the form of obedience and even creating a bond with the abuser. This is frequently known as Stockholm Syndrome or trauma-bond. This occurs when a person is subjected to long-term emotional. psychological and/or physical abuse. In order to survive, the victim bonds with their abuser, similar to when a child bonds with their abusive parent. The parent is the child's only caregiver and in order to live, the child tries to appease and make them happy to avoid further abuse. The narcissist praises the victim and promises the world. Then they use the victims' insecurities against them. This is where you become an easy target for the emotional, psychological and financial abuse while the cycle continues. Once they have you on the hook, they drain your energy, love, zest for life, money and resources all for themselves. This is why it's important to heal your inner wounds so you don't attract energy vampires. However, some personalities lend themselves even more to narcissists.

Empaths, Co-Dependents and Co-Narcissists

What is the difference between being empathetic and being an empath? Someone who is empathetic gives appropriate responses to life events like new births, funerals and graduations. They can place themselves in the person's shoes and give appropriate responses. Who is an empath? Empath is a term used to identify someone who also is empathetic but they take it to a deeper level. They can actually take on the other person's energy and feelings as if they were going through it themselves. Aside from dealing with their own emotions, trying to manage others feelings leaves them emotionally and energetically drained. They also want to make others happy sometimes at their own expense. Empaths are similar to co-dependents because they tend to be people pleasers. Unlike a co-dependent, empaths may not support irresponsible behavior and can set boundaries. Making others happy is part of the nature of an empath (Reynolds 2019) Link. They are the complete opposite of the narcissists.

Who is a co-narcissist? According to therapist Christine L. De Cannonville, a co-narcissist is someone who survived trauma and abuse as a child from a narcissistic parent. In order to survive, they believed the only way to feel validated, loved and supported was to give into and validate the narcissist instead. Creating a bond with the abuser who took care of them increased their chances at survival. In the case with the narcissist, opposites attract but not for the well-being of the empaths, codependents or co-narcissists.. According to Christiane Northrup in her book Dodging Energy Vampires, empaths become very good at blending in and figuring out how to be loved and accepted not for who they really are, but instead for how they can serve others. Empaths are highly intuitive to other people's energies. They show great compassion for others. They feel the weight of the world. They will do whatever it takes to make the relationship work. They see good and best in others. Usually they are introverts or prefer being alone. They may suffer fatigue, especially being around other people, because empaths feel all the energy, whether good or bad, they just feel it. If empaths are not careful and don't protect their energy, they just take on the energy around them. On the other side of the spectrum, empaths usually achieve high levels of success in life like becoming doctors, CEOs, managers, leaders in industry, lawyers, etc. They are premium energy and targets for energy vampires.

Getting Hooked

So how do narcissists get such smart, intelligent, nice people? What hooks victims in? The energy vampires are master manipulators. They become the dream person the target victim wishes and yearns for. In the beginning stages of a relationship, they "love bomb" you by telling you how wonderful, beautiful, smart, accomplished, talented, you are. They make you feel like you are the one and only love of their life. You are the long lost soulmate, as if they have been waiting for you all their lives. They magically have everything a victim ever wanted in a love partner. The narcissist reads their victims and molds themselves to mirror the "dream" image, like a Ken or Barbie doll. They make you feel like you are the most important person in the world by buying you gifts and spending all their free time with you. You think to yourself, "Wow, this is the person I have been waiting for all my life." They promise you the world. They become who you want them to be, the perfect soulmate. Without realizing it, you just fall right into their hook and before you know it, you are in love. At first, they make you feel like you are also their perfect person. You feel right at home with the energy vampire. However, they're not in it for you or for what's best for you. They don't deliver on their promises. This is how you can start to understand who they are. They start gaslighting you as soon as they feel you are secure in their grip.

Gas lighting

What is gas lighting? When I think of the term, I think of a cigarette lighter. The term is best explained in a film called Gaslight, based on a play written in 1938 by Patrick Hamilton. It is based on a young naive woman who witnesses the murder of her aunt, whose home she later inherits. She meets and marries a dashing man in Italy and they move into her home. Shortly thereafter, she begins to hear knocking on the walls and the gas light dim in her lamp. Her husband tells her she's imagining things. In addition, he makes her believe she is forgetful and acting in strange ways. Slowly, the young woman begins to doubt her own sanity. He confines her to the home by telling people she is not well. The term is derived from this film. It is defined when a person lies for their own gain to another person so repeatedly and with so much confidence that the victim begins to doubt their own sanity. As the victim doubts his or her own reality and own judgement, he or she becomes more dependent and trusts their gas lighter more than they trust themselves (Wilkinson 2017) Link. Gaslighting is psychological manipulation based on fears and doubts of the victim. Energy vampires are experts at gaslighting. First, they make you feel like they love you unconditionally with all your flaws. Then the next minute they make you feel like you don't know what you're talking about. This is very confusing for the victim and in order to keep the peace, they deny their own gut, intuition, and evidence gathered or discovered. It's a very tormenting situation because the victim does not want to accept the fact that the love of their life is now the monster from their worst nightmares.

In my situation, my second husband was an extreme narcissist. Initially, he made me feel like I was the next best thing to a Rolls Royce. He lavished me with compliments, acts of service and gifts. He wanted to be with me all the time. He was funny and charming. He told me everything I wanted to hear. He hit on the things I wanted from a man. Literally, he checked off all my boxes. I thought I had hit the jackpot. Soon after, he made me question my appearance, social behavior, and my entire being in order to feel better about himself. He made me feel less than him through his snide comments and so called "jokes." He would make me feel even more awkward in social settings and then accuse me of being overly sensitive. He would make me feel like what I said was dumb, stupid or didn't make sense. He also used my faith as a way to manipulate me. He used God's word to say God told him we would be married. Later he used the bible to say my primary duty was to meet his needs. He even manipulated and psychologically tortured me by saying that if he wasn't sexually satisfied then he might fall into temptation, placing the blame on me as if it was my fault.

Even though I was the breadwinner and took care of everything, I mean everything, he still discredited all of my contributions and hard work. He would guilt trip me for working, even though he could not afford nor did he want to pay the bills. He told me he wanted to be a minister and he knew I wanted to marry a pastor. Later, he made me feel unworthy or that I wasn't living up to the standards of the faith. He even accused me as the reason why he left the church. He blamed me for his behavior. When I brought things to his attention, he pointed the finger at me. He acted like a great leader, father and role model in public, but at home he was quite the opposite. He would say that the pastor agreed with him and that I was the one that needed to change. I would end up believing him and apologizing.

They make out the truth to be a lie and the lie to be the truth. You often end up taking the blame and the guilt because you want to keep the peace. Actually, accepting the truth is more painful. They stand behind their lies as God's truth. For victims of abuse, the old subconscious patterns kick in and they just take on the blame and the guilt. Victims of abuse have difficulty believing in themselves and what is true. We freeze and can not make decisions for ourselves so we just believe what they say and accept it. We can not handle the friction (dissonance) and we avoid confrontation. We either have to accept what they say or leave. In cases of trauma-bonding, you don't want to leave. We can not leave because our body is actually addicted to the environment. That is correct! The body is addicted to abuse, also known as trauma-bonding. I will cover this in more detail in chapter 6.

Let's talk about how the law of vibration affects the cycles of abuse. First, understand we attract the energy that is inside of us and the frequency will attract more of the same. Those unhealed wounds and unhealed traumas will continue to play out. Even if we can get away, we will continue to attract this type of person and we will continue to let them use and abuse us in many different ways. You do things you never thought you would do. You never thought you would allow someone to do to you what you accept from an energy vampire. Your subconscious patterns and beliefs will allow you to unconsciously accept being abused. If you continue in a relationship with an energy vampire, they will continue to drain your energy, life and money. Aside from psychological abuse, they abuse you financially. Depleting your savings and maxing out your credit cards. You find yourself taking out loans, signing for additional debt to appease and make him or her happy. They want a nice house and car. They want to travel and you do whatever it takes to make it happen. You want to make them happy to avoid conflict. When you are being gaslighted, they are playing up all your fears and doubts. They place you in a fight or flight mode, never knowing when the next attack will come that you compromise even your personal values. You question yourself and your self-worth. You take on their guilt and shame. You begin to think there is something wrong with you and not him/her. You apologize profusely as you find yourself continuously taking the blame when they're the ones doing the wrong. If you do not get out of the relationship, you may suffer permanent damage to your mind, body and spirit. These abusers do not care about you. It's all about them. They strip you of basic human rights to safety and freedom.

Even in the midst of lies and cheating, you may still protect him or her to make an appearance as if everything is good. You deny that you're in an abusive relationship even to yourself. You cannot fathom the thought of letting others know what is happening to you. If you stay, eventually you will not be able to function with all that stress and anxiety. The more you give, the less you get and the more abuse is pounded upon you.

In my situation, as my income increased, he would make me feel guilty. He would not say "Congratulations!" He would just give me a blank stare when I shared my accomplishments. He would then find ways to gaslight me to feel better about himself.

If you continue with the relationship, your body will eventually give out. Your adrenals will be unable to balance as you continue to go down spirals. It will be very difficult to recover from the hormonal imbalance. You may even need permanent psychotic drugs to function. You won't be able to perform normal work activities or home duties. You can place yourself at risk for losing your job, home, car, family, and friends. This resembles the behavior of someone addicted to drugs. You still continue to go back to that person. You cannot see yourself living without him or her. This all goes back to the trauma-bond in your body you have not healed. You will rationalize your way out of leaving. The effects of these long term patterns include unexplained physical ailments like auto-immune diseases. During stress or PTSD, your immune system is suppressed. You can have emotional breakdowns, energetic drainage and depression. You're unable to sleep and carry a poor self-image of yourself. You have no self-love and you end up losing yourself to the other person. You give up on your own dreams. You pursue their happiness and dreams. The debt you incur can lead to bankruptcy, financial losses and you believe you deserve it. You believe the reason why all these things are happening is because you did something wrong. The after effects are very, very painful and can continue for the rest of your life, if you don't heal your inner wounds. When you have nothing else to give or if you start to heal yourself, the energy vampire will discard you. By then, he or she has already moved on to the next victim. They jump from one person to the next without a second thought, remorse or regret. They move on at the drop of a hat because they never really cared or loved you.

It is a very difficult reality to accept because you gave up your life for that person. It is hard to accept and let go. You may start stalking them on social media. You hope and pray they come back to you. You may even beg them to come back. All because you just cannot break free from the trauma-bond. We will explore how to break yourself free from trauma-bonding in chapter 6. It begins with healing your inner childhood traumas.

In my experience, when I took a step back, I had to face the reality that I was married to an energy vampire. I divorced my first narcissistic husband only to marry another narcissist. I realized that all of my previous relationships were with narcissists. It all went back to when I was a young girl when I experienced the trauma. My abuser was a narcissist, so evil and incapable of remorse or feelings of regret. These experiences led to trauma-bonding and codependency. My life revolved around making other people happy and giving my all to them so that I could receive love, affection and happiness. Narcissists pray and live off of people like me, they get their energy and feed their egos from codependent people. I was a giver and he was a taker, the ying/yang. Towards the end, he was accusing me of cheating while all along he was the one cheating. Within a week of moving out, I found an opened condom wrapper in my convertible BMW while I stayed in a women's shelter. I gave him everything and the more I gave, the more emotional abuse and trauma I received. I constantly accepted the lies, cheating, verbal, emotional and psychological abuse. On a subconscious level I accepted it because I didn't think I deserved better. I was repeating the patterns over and over again. I thought this was normal. I thought this was how all men were and I couldn't change that fact. He reinforced this belief by telling me "yea, all men are dogs." I just accepted it as I had accepted my childhood abuse. My "job" was to make sure my man was happy no matter what. He is an expert manipulator using God's word to perpetuate his self-serving agenda.

I upheld the standards of my faith. I didn't realize this was not normal. God didn't want me to live this way. I didn't understand I mattered and my happiness was most important. I didn't know I had a right to be happy or how to be happy. I continued to accept things I never thought I would accept. I didn't believe I deserved any better. I continued in the cycle of abuse until I dealt with my emotional pain. What have you accepted into your life that does not support or fulfill you?

CHAPTER 5

Is There Any Hope for a Happy Life?

The good news is, yes, there is hope. However, you have to break free from the cycles of abuse and trauma-bonding. The bad news is that it's not going to be easy, similar to when an addict cannot control their tendency to continue to use their drug of choice. When your subconscious mind becomes used to the cycles of abuse and negative self-talk, it's almost impossible to leave on your own. The terror of finding out your significant other is cheating on you or abusing you, causes you to stay quiet and pretend everything is ok. The trauma from childhood created a subconscious pattern the body remembers and becomes more easily addicted during trauma-bonding with a new abuser.

What is Trauma-Bonding?

So what is trauma-bonding? Here you go, our thoughts create peptides that run through all of our cells. Those same peptides that are floating in your body in large quantities are what your body becomes addicted to. Your body or subconscious patterns will literally push you to return to the abuser in a similar situation in order to satisfy the craving. Even if you leave the abuser, you will find another person who does the same without even realizing it. In order to break free, you have to heal our inner deep wounds stemming from childhood. This is the only way to go from surviving to thriving and becoming free from the cycles of abuse for good. Once free from trauma-bond, you will not go back to the abuser like a drug addict looking for more of the same. Trauma-bonding is why such a high percentage of women go back to their abusers and remain until they are discarded or worse, until they are gone from this earth. If they are discarded, they go back or find another person who will do the same.

Trauma Bond	Authentic Love
"I need you" "I'm addicted to you"	"I see you" "I hear you"
Highs + lows (nervous system activation) as connection	Mutual trust, predictable, words align with actions
Emotionally phobic, but highly sexual	Emotionally vulnerable, open communication
Enables behavior that is harmful, deceitful, or abusive to receive love	Has clear boundaries, free of self betrayal, values accountability
Partner's attempt to mold and/or control each other	Partner's do inner work to hold space to grow + evolve

@the.holistic.psychologist

Finding Your Self-Love, Self-Worth and Value

How do you find your value, self-worth and self-love? It is very important to love yourself more than the other person or anyone else.

This is not easy when you were never taught how to love yourself as a child. Perhaps your parents did not show you love or gave you affirmation. You're not even aware you're not loving yourself by accepting less than you deserve. I thought I loved myself, but I really was not loving myself when I allowed the abuse and poor treatment in my life. Do a test to see if you really love yourself. It also strengthens your self-love. Look at yourself in the mirror. Look straight into your eyes and say the following. Place your name where my name is in this case. "Selene, I love you. I really, really love you. You are the love of my life and I will never leave you. I will always honor, cherish and respect you all the days of my life." Try saying that to yourself several times in front of the mirror. Can you say it without breaking? How do you feel when you say it? How do you react to it? Did you cry? I know I cried and many others when we first said it aloud to ourselves. I first learned it from Bird Mejia, my life coach and mentor. Keep saying it to yourself every time you are in front of the mirror at work or out. Repeat it many times in the morning when you are getting ready and in the evening before bedtime. Once you can say it without breaking, that is a good indicator your self-love is growing. Just keep repeating it over and over, every chance you get. The more you say it out loud, the more you will believe it and the more love you will feel for yourself. In order to remove toxic people and toxic thoughts from your being, you have to love and heal yourself.

There are a lot of techniques to increase your self-love, self-worth and value. It will require a lot of work and repetition. Say to yourself out loud or in your mind, "I am loved. I am enough. I am perfect," over and over throughout the day. Journal by writing it out on paper with a pen, which makes it real. Say affirmations to yourself as you're working, driving and going about your day. Repeat them before you go to bed and when you wake up, especially during theta state. If tears come out, let them flow, don't stop them. There is healing in tears. Be there for yourself, close your eyes and give yourself a hug. Imagine your little inner child crying on your shoulder and you are consoling him or her. Tell your inner child that you will never, ever leave or abandon him or her again.

You want to stay with your feelings and embrace them, even if you feel like you're going to die. Trust me, you will not die, you already survived the real worst event. Even if it feels like you won't make it through, you will. Stay strong and hold on to your feelings. This is also known as self-partnering. You want to process through your emotions by journaling, talking about them to a trusted confidant or counselor. Find out what false beliefs you created about yourself when you went through the trauma, so you can change them for positive beliefs about yourself. The negative beliefs are trapped in your subconscious mind, so you can not retrieve the memories on command. You have to dig deep through layers and layers. Placing yourself in theta state helps you retrieve the old data more easily. This state also helps to rewrite your new programming. When you are in this state you more readily accept thoughts as truth and engrave your subconscious mind. The theta state is a great opportunity to rewrite your old disk (subconscious patterns) with new beliefs about yourself. Theta state is achieved between that little space in time between when you're half awake and half asleep. This is the reason why people pray and meditate with their eyes closed and in a very relaxed position. It is also a great time to affirm yourself with positive thoughts and how you see yourself in the future. It is crucial to see yourself happy, full of joy and free from all the toxicity and negativity.

In my first vision board, I pasted pictures of serenity, laughter and peace. I did not add material things like cars, homes or other things. I had those things already and they didn't bring me joy. I wanted happiness to come in abundance from the inside out, instead of the outside in. At the time, I was living in a women's shelter. I had two homes I owned, but I left them in order to get the peace and serenity I desperately needed. I set an image of my new life in my heart and mind. I looked at my vision board daily to help change my thoughts of how I saw myself until it became a reality.

In order to change our old paradigms, we need to constantly think and write out the new patterns until the thoughts become part of our new way of living. Once you start noticing positive patterns without your prompting, you will know your new subconscious patterns are becoming part of your new identity. In order to change our subconscious beliefs, we have to change the way we think about ourselves. We want to bring those horrific actions to light. As they are coming up, write them down. Write down what you are feeling in your body. Ask yourself, how far back does it go? When did it start? What was the scenario? What was I experiencing at the time? You will be surprised at what comes up when you give yourself permission to go back without any judgement. Soon after, without prompting, you will go back to that time when you were abused or had the traumatic event. You will start to remember the thoughts and feelings that crossed your mind at the time. In those moments you can capture the false beliefs you created and believed about yourself. Beliefs such as, "I am not lovable," "I am not worthy of love," "I am not beautiful," etc. You can change the beliefs once you process through those emotions. The emotions can include anger, grief, disbelief and many other emotions. It is ok to allow yourself the time needed to process and journal through all of that stuff. It also really helps to have someone you trust to listen to you and help you through the process. You can call them accountability partners or someone with a similar background to yours. I have created an online coaching program to help walk you through this process as well on my website at www.selenelifecoach.com. You do not have to do this alone. I am also available as a coach to help you. Once you release the pain, you can reprogram your old thoughts with new healthy beliefs about yourself. You can make room for your new healthy way of being and your new happy life! I promise you if you work hard and don't give up, you too can achieve freedom, happiness and success. We have the same light and abilities. You can do whatever I can do and many other women who have turned their lives around.

Look at Tina Turner, if you do not know who she is, look her up on YouTube. She is a world famous singer with so much energy and life. She came from a broken home. Her parents constantly fought and eventually split. They abandoned Tina and her sister to their grandmother who raised them near Memphis, TN. Tina always knew she wanted to sing and when she met Ike Turner, her first husband, he gave her the chance to sing. He was already a well known singer with a band. According to an interview with Larry King Live (1997), Ike treated her very well in the beginning. She was still in high school when she saw him sing for the first time. He let her sing one night and when he saw how the audience responded, he made her a singer in his band. She loved it. The duo had hit songs like 'A Fool in Love" ranked #2. They had a total of 10 hit songs. Behind closed doors, when the lights and show were over; however, Tina was taking beatings by Ike. When he asked Tina to marry him to secure his "investment," he took her to Tijuana, Mexico to tie the knot. For their honeymoon, he took her to a brothel. This really hurt Tina, but it was only the beginning of a marriage full of physical and emotional abuse. He became very controlling of her life and career. She always went along and agreed to do things Ike's way for fear of getting a broken nose, jaw or an awful beating. He even threw hot coffee on her face once.

At age 29, Tina almost took her a life with an overdose of sleeping pills because she could not take the pain anymore. When she made it through, she realized she had a purpose on earth and decided to live. While she was in the hospital recovering, Ike told her she should have died. Almost 10 years later and after 20 years of abuse, badly beaten up, she finally mustered enough courage to escape with thirty-six cents in her pocket and a gas card. She was almost 40 years old. She begged a hotel clerk to let her spend her first night there and he allowed her. She wanted nothing from Ike, only her freedom and her name. She struggled for 2 years on her own. However, she went through her own healing journey and came out a stronger, more brilliant super star than she was before, full of courage and wisdom. She became known as the Queen of Rock & Roll with more than 200 million records sold. She had many more hit singles like "What's Love Got to Do with It." In her memoir called "I Tina," she shared how her intimate relationships with Ike, were like rape. She was beaten up before and/or after. Ike admitted to beating her up as if it was normal. He himself came from an abusive childhood, but became a narcissist instead. He eventually overdosed on drugs. Tina's memoir later became a movie of her life titled "What's Love Got to Do with It." I highly recommend this movie if you have not seen it but have a box of tissues next to you. Tina did find peace, love and happiness after she divorced. She met a very loving and supporting man named Erwin Bach, who even donated one of his kidneys to her. She had a lot of health issues including cancer, high blood pressure, stroke and other ailments (Haynes 2020) Link. Her story demonstrates for us that even after the most horrific abuse, we can still achieve our dreams and success after we heal. Tina found her self-worth, value and self-love.

Self-Healing

Everyone's journey is different. You have to find what works for you. However, the most important part is to change your old paradigms, the false beliefs about yourself. Change the old patterns for new ones, where you are happy, loving yourself and living your dreams. The law of attraction will bring it to you. There are various steps to this process and I will review how to free yourself from trauma-bonding in more detail in the next chapter. Here is the process in a nutshell: Visualization helped me the most where I held my pain and then released it, seeing it escaping my body. I was never able to let it go before, even though I tried. After it leaves my body, I receive a beautiful bright light from above, from life source, energy, God, whatever it is to you. I continue to allow the light in, through all of my cells, replacing the empty space where the old traumatic memories used to live. Bringing those traumatic terrible thoughts and feelings to light, feeling them in full strength and then releasing them, has been the most effective way for me to heal. The Philosophical Tree an essay from psychologist CG Hung says, "One does not become enlightened by imagining figures of light, but by making the darkness conscious. The latter procedure, however, is disagreeable and therefore not popular." Before letting the light in, I had to acknowledge the pain. Afterwards, I let the light in and allowed it to fill me with love and acceptance. This process has been a life changer. Each hold and release is not longer than a few minutes, but it has taken me a long time to release all of the thoughts and feelings I had bottled up. Especially in my case, I had a lot of traumatic events to release so it took me longer. However, after each release, I started to feel better instantly knowing I received an instant healing. It is a continuous process and I work through it whenever I need to. This is how I started my mornings. It made a world of difference when I didn't abandon myself. As a child, I felt abandoned by my parents and I continued to abandon myself whenever I would feel pain or had a bad memory come to mind.

Before my healing journey, I was miserable my entire life. Even though on the surface, everything looked good, I pretended everything was fine. I was taught as a child, no matter what happened, everything was fine. Despite this, I was able to have a thriving career, even though I struggled on the inside. I had a "good marriage" with step kids. I finished my undergraduate and master's degrees in business. I was making good money, more than I ever dreamed before. My ex-husband and I were leaders in our church. I worked out, I ate healthy. However, I could not enjoy life. I was still angry at the world and I lived in isolation. I bottled my emotions and never spoke my truth or what I wanted. I continued to stay super busy, so I would not deal with my pain. I kept ignoring it and running away from myself. It took a lot for me to realize and open my eyes to what I was doing and what I had accepted in my life. I even ended up in a woman's shelter, so ashamed and afraid of everything. I left my ex-husband and left everything to him. Sometimes, you have to cut your losses in order to live a better life.

Everything was surreal in the beginning stages of the honeymoon phase. Little by little, my ex became an abuser. Towards the end, he started to escalate his angry behavior by breaking things and destroying our property. He was calling me names trying to shame and guilt me for his problems. He was engulfing me via texts and accusing me of cheating. He was out of control using drugs and abusing me. I had to call the police for help one night and then I felt guilty because he was arrested. I apologized profusely but I did what I needed to do for me to feel safe. I eventually recognized the patterns of abuse, after I started healing. I had support to leave him and so I did. I managed the courage because I knew if I stayed it would lead to an emotional breakdown or worse. However, I continued a relationship with him, even from a distance. He manipulated me with promises of change and love. I managed to keep working and trying to keep everything seemingly as normal as I could. I still lived in isolation and in pain. I was in denial of my pain, but I knew I had to do something about it. I had to change something in my life, but I just had no idea how.

I often prayed to God to take my life because I didn't find joy or happiness on this earth. However, I felt in my heart from God that I had a purpose and I was going to help others. I found comfort in the thought. I held on to that belief, that what I was going through was not in vain. I drove all over the city and suburbs learning and listening to everything and everyone that I could learn from. I had to figure out what was wrong with me and how my life got to where it was. I learned so much from different people and different sources. I dedicated all of my spare time to learning how to break free and find peace. Until I found the answers I was looking for. I want you to know you are not alone and there are many thousands of men and women on this journey with you. It will require determination and dedication on your part. Do it for your children and your family. When you heal yourself, you also heal seven generations before and after you. You can break free from abuse and its long term effects.

CHAPTER 6

Free Yourself from Trauma Bonding

What is it? When I first heard the term, I wondered if I suffered from it. I could not believe this was the cause of the cycle of abuse that repeated itself in my life over and over again. These cycles were caused by chemical addictions in my body. Feelings of abandonment create peptides that run through our entire body. When our cells constantly receive this flow, they become used to it. Eventually, the body will crave and want more of the same without realizing it. You look for those situations or people that create the effects of the rushes associated with abandonment, separation and victim mentality. For example, take someone who loves sugar. If they try to go without it, they cannot stop thinking about it. The more they want to stop, the more they crave it until they give in. Then they feel guilty and start shaming their body. This is an addictive cycle, not only for the sugar itself, but also for the shaming afterwards. He or she will find comfort in self-loathing and pity. Without realizing it, you attract more of the same and stay in this vicious cycle.

In Dr. Bruce Lipton's book called Biology of Belief, he explains how cells have receptors like antennae that react to not only instructions from our brain, but our thoughts and also our environment like sound, light and radio frequencies. They change the behavior of our cells to an appropriate response (Lipton 2015) Link. Sound familiar, remember epigenetics? The environmental stimuli, including thoughts, create biological behavior in our cells just like physical stimuli. This fact provides for pharmaceutical-free energy healing medicine. The epigenetics from childhood propel the thoughts and beliefs that continue to shape our current and future state. This is why it is so important to change and heal the emotional trauma and beliefs we created. The cells' membrane is semi-permeable and controls the cells more than the nucleus. Dr. Lipton further uncovered how we can reprogram our cells with information from our environment. Thank goodness it is not solely based on our genes from birth. The receptors and effectors in our cells' membranes act as the Central Processing Unit (CPU), like the brain of a computer. Bob Proctor further explains how our body is energy, "We are changing at a rate of 50 million cells per second. Our thoughts create the energy that flows through our body." The neuropeptide amino acid chains found in all our cells get hooked or addicted to the ones they receive regular rushes of. If we regularly experience victimization and feelings of powerlessness associated with abuse, our brain will push us to the source of that neuropeptide to interact with it. This creates a trauma-bond that you cannot escape from with your own regular thoughts or freewill. According to Melanie Tonya Evans' book called "You can Thrive After Narcissistic Abuse," she uses scientific research using lab rats to illustrate how our cells can get addicted to neuropeptides. The rats are fed neuropeptides along with their regular diet. Shortly thereafter, the rats forgo food, water and self-care in order to obtain the peptide. The peptides are more addictive than any other synthetic drug. Can you believe that! They are more addictive than any other synthetic drug. More addicting than heroin, crack, marijuana, you name it.

New Revelation

This powerful revelation blew my mind away. This is why I could not leave my recent abuser as easily. This is why I kept attracting more of the same and making excuses to stay. This is why I was trapped in a vicious cycle that I could not get away from or stop. I thought it was the other person, so I removed him. I divorced my first husband and got remarried soon after. I did not give myself time to heal. The problem or addiction was inside of me, in my body. I remarried the same type of narcissist. Until I healed those inner wounds from childhood, I was finally able to break free from the trauma-bonding in order to experience peace and joy.

Your brain follows your body. So what does that mean? In order to think better, you must feel better first when you have unhealed wounds. It is a decision you have to make. The body will find any excuse to go back and get more of the same drug. You will make excuses as to why you need to stay in an abusive relationship. You will rationalize it. You will live in denial until it comes to light. You will hide it from friends and family.

I know I hid it all from friends and family. I lived in isolation and only I knew how I felt. I didn't want to burden anyone with my problems and instead I focused on other people's problems. Once I realized what was happening, I started to immediately do the necessary work. I started my healing journey because I knew if I didn't then there would be nothing left of me. I would not survive more trauma in my life. It was getting towards the end and I could not function with a clear head at work. I could not sleep peacefully. I remember one night my ex terrified me. It was out of this world, literally. I had to play along just so I could lay down and try to get some rest. The situation was dire and chaotic. I told myself this was not how I wanted to live my life. Once I started healing, I started to feel better and have more peace in my life.

Breaking Free

So how do you break free? The first thing is to free your mind! There are many ways of changing your subconscious patterns, paradigms and self-beliefs. I follow many people to learn different methods and techniques. There is prayer, affirmations, EFT tapping, mantras, healing meditations, healing your chakras, healing vibrations, hertz 432 sounds and more. My favorite was Melanie Tonya Evans' healing program. I learned that by self-partnering and going inward, I can start to heal. If I focus on the external symptoms, then I cannot truly heal. Quantum Law that states so within so without, how we feel inside is what we create outside. We can begin to understand that if we try to control others, we give our power away. However, by holding ourselves through the pain of traumatic events and past traumas, we can begin to process the pain and file it away. We begin to live from our true selves and true beliefs. When you begin to heal, you will be on your healing journey, little by little, layer by layer, you will start to lose the triggering effects of what has happened to you. You will be able to change the belief you hold about yourself and find your self-worth and self-love. There are many methods to change your subconscious patterns. The most important aspect is to change them. Pick a few different ones that resonate with you to find the one or several that work best for you, depending on your comfort level. You can never have too many tools in your shed. You never know when you will need them. I will highlight two in this book.

EFT Tapping

EFT tapping involves tapping yourself in specific places on your body called meridian points. Studies at Harvard University have shown that stimulating these points can significantly reduce the levels of activity in the amygdala. The amygdala is like an alarm system that floods our bodies with cortisol during trauma or fear. In another study, Dr. Dawson Church had three groups. The first one received EFT tapping for an hour. The second group had a talking session with a counselor and the third had no treatment at all. He measured the cortisol level of these three groups. The first group with EFT tapping had a reduction from 50% to 20% percent less cortisol in the body. While in comparison the second group had little to no reduction in cortisol levels. The second group walked out with just as much stress as when they walked in even though they talked about it.

During EFT tapping, we start by stating out loud what we're feeling while tapping our meridian points. The most common meridian points are the side of hand, corner of eyebrow, next to eyes, underneath the eye, underneath the nose, between lip and chin, right underneath the collarbone, underneath the armpit and top of the head. You start by saying "even though I feel sad, I deeply and completely accept myself and how I feel." It could be sadness, feelings abandoned, or any trigger from childhood. While tapping, you start to change the words you say outloud to positive safe words, thoughts and feelings. Thereby reprogramming your thoughts and feelings around a particular memory or thought that brings you stress. It works on so many other different things like weight loss, self-image, money and health issues. By reducing the levels of cortisol during the repetition through the meridian points, we deactivate the fight or flight mode. We change the feelings of being unsafe to feelings of safety and acceptance. You change how you feel and start to feel better. It is important to note, we are accepting and acknowledging the negative feeling and not running away from it. While you verbalize how you are feeling, you can start to change from a negative thought to a positive thought during the EFT

Process (Tapping 2020) Link. You can also watch YouTube videos on how to apply EFT tapping to different situations. There are several for anxiety, fear associated with PTSD and so many more.

According to Dr. Lissa Rankin, author of Mind Over Medicine, during EFT, you release healing hormones and activate self-repair mechanisms. She also believes the mind has the power to heal our bodies much like the placebo effect (American Riviera 2012) Link.

When I tried EFT tapping, it certainly helped me feel better. What worked best for me? Healing the thriver way! By using visualization during theta state and reaching my subconscious memories, I hold and release the pain.

Healing the Thriver Way - Visualization

We can reach our subconscious mind more easily by closing our eyes and sitting or lying in a relaxed state. Start by asking your body what part is hurting or feeling pain? Without any judgment or denying whatever comes up, keep an open mind and let the thoughts flow in a natural way. Then ask the body or pain, what is it that is causing the pain or discomfort? Listen empathetically and encourage the story to unfold. Let your body and mind tell you what is causing the pain. Write it down and give it a rating from one to ten. One being hardly feel it at all to 10 being the most troublesome. Then hold on to the feelings associated with that memory. As hard and scary as it may feel, hold on to the thoughts and do let your mind wonder. Do not excuse the thoughts or dismiss them away. Then on paper and using a pen write it out. Write out what you are feeling and let it flow for about a minute. Then close your eyes again, feeling the pain to the max, let it build to its capacity. Then after feeling it to the max, see a tornado turning inside your body. Let the feelings of pain, anxiety, powerlessness, victimization, and the like, build within the tornado and release them from the top of your head. See the tornado and all the "dark and heavy" matter and feelings leaving your physical body and going back to nothingness, turning into love. Keep releasing all of the tornado until you feel clear from those feelings. Visualize the pain and all that trauma you were feeling just leave your body. Know that you do not have to resolve the issues. God, the universe or your source of light will take care of everything. Then go to your most favorite place where you feel peace, love and joy. My place is on a warm, sunny beach with the sun shining and the water sloshing beneath my toes. Clear aqua marine blue skies and white puffy clouds surround me. The crystal clear water and the white sand between my toes, fill me with so much support and love. Take a deep breath in and see the heavens open up and the light shine down on you. The light from a great source of power, God or the universe, enters your body through the crown of your head filling every cell with its light. Every cell in your body gets filled with so much light and love. You then start to radiate the bright warm sun light all around you until the entire beach is filled with your light. Then invite your younger versions of yourself to join you. In my case, my little girl always shows up. Embrace all of them sharing your love and light. Then see angels or other higher beings coming around you and your younger selves, taking out the rest of the darkness and trauma inside of you, turning it all into love. The angels also switch on your genes and all your cells to receive more light. The light continues to fill you until everyone is glowing and filling up the beach and surroundings with your radiant light, shining bright for all to see. Know for certain that you have received an instant healing. Your body knows how to retain the healing. Now you can move on with your life full of love and ready to receive more of the same. Melanie Tonia Evans does amazing work walking us through this process. It is incredible how this shift can change everything. I know it did for me. It cleared my traumas, including the ones from when I was a little girl. It gave me so much power, control and determination to change my environment and my life to where I am today. You see it is not our deepest fear we are afraid of, but our light.

"Our worst fear is not that we are inadequate. Our deepest fear is that we are powerful beyond measure. It is our light, not our darkness, that most frightens us. We asked ourselves, 'Who am I to be brilliant, gorgeous, talented, fabulous?' Actually, who are you not to be? You are a child of God. Your playing small, does not serve the world. There is nothing enlightened about shrinking so that other people won't feel insecure around you. We were born to manifest the glory of God within us. It's not just in some of us; it's everyone. And as we let our light shine, we unconsciously give other people permission to do the same. As we are liberated from our own fear, our presence automatically liberates others." A poem by Marianne Williamson author of several books including "The Gift of Change" and "A Return to Love."

In order to change our behavior, we have to start with our thoughts. In order to change our thoughts, we have to change our subconscious patterns and paradigms we learned in our childhood. You can break the cycle of abuse by healing the roots. I urge you to go back in time to discover what created those negative paradigms about yourself that lead to addictive peptides. What is a paradigm you might ask? According to Bob Proctor, "A paradigm is multiple attitudes we learned from childhood both positive and negative. An image of self built as a child and is the habitual way of living." It is this original trauma that keeps causing the addiction. Just like those peptides ran through our body during the first abuse, our subconscious mind remembers it. When healing, you are replacing those peptides and awful memories with positive ones. Examine your life and see if this resonates with you. This explains why you're not able to free yourself or stay away from your abuser as much as you want to. You would never go back to look for more victimization under normal circumstances. People that have not suffered abuse as a child, do not tolerate or fall prey to abuse or narcissists' ploys because they did not experience it or have any similar peptides in their body.

The most important goal is to find out what works best for you. Seek help or work with someone who has been through what you have been through. Heal the thriver way with visualization. Once you heal the trauma, there is no hook left for the narcissist. There is nothing to keep going back to in the peptide addiction. The body doesn't have to look for more of the same and the cravings simply vanish. The addictions to peptides just disappear. They dissolve away, the cravings are gone. We can not think our way out of our large goldmines. We have to go inwards to our body and emotions. Emotions are energy in motion all over our body. Healing the trauma-bond and chemical addictions will set us free. Toxic people will not find any more energy within you to keep coming back for more. Once you heal, you will start to operate at a higher frequency. You will attract positive minded and happy people.

Hundreds of thousands of people have been freed from trauma-bonding and been able to once again achieve the freedom they have a right to enjoy. They go on to live the life they dreamed of and not only survive but thrive in life. They recover what they lost and receive it back in abundance. Finding financial freedom, love, peace, joy and happiness are but a few examples. They also achieve success in careers and win divorce and child custody court battles. Healing yourself will stop the manipulation. Best of all, you won't go back for more. I encourage you to go without contact with your abuser. If you can not due to shared custody, then modify contact to not feed them any more of your time or energy. Stay drama free.

This will also give you the ability to stand up for yourself and not allow their tactics to work on you any longer. You will find self-love and you won't compromise your values by allowing any more abuse into your life.

Breaking away with all five senses from your abuser is important in your healing journey. No contact can be accomplished by blocking numbers, email addresses, social media, and reducing contact with anyone who brings their message. Sometimes they use other family members, children or leaders to speak to you on their behalf. Do not accept any of it and hold your boundaries. Once you heal, you will not even want an apology. Don't worry, you will never receive one from a narcissist. They will never take accountability or accept blame or fault. If you have to maintain contact because of children or working with a boss then use modified contact. During modified contact, only focus on the facts and what you need to deal with them about and that's it. Do not feed into the drama or give them any energy. They will always try to suck you into an argument or try to make you feel guilty. Just cut them off, don't feed into it, ignore them and move on. These people never change. They don't take responsibility for their actions and they always blame you. They make you out to be the bad person in the relationship and smear your name to friends and family. The best comeback is to cut off your supply of energy and go live your best life without them!

Healing from trauma-bonding has now given me new freedom and opened up the world. I didn't understand why I kept going back and accepting things I knew not to accept. I could not stop myself. Trauma-bonding, I discovered, is a deep biological addiction. Far more addictive than any substance abuse. My body literally craved the adrenal rushes from the cycle of abuse. It was like waking up from a horrible nightmare. I remember when I was little, I used to watch black and white movies like Frankenstein and The Count Dracula. These movies were very scary to me at the time. The vampire would affix his eyes on his victim and hypnotize her. The victim would be powerless to escape and was drawn to the vampire during a sleepwalking hypnosis. She would walk up to the vampire and allow him to suck all the blood he wanted, leaving her lifeless. Then the vampire would move on to the next victim. This is a good illustration of what happens when an unhealed person is around an energy vampire. The conditioning or epigenetics from childhood, make the person an easy meal for them. The victim is not even aware of what is going on until it's too late. The cycles include the honeymoon phase, the explosion, the makeup, and repeat. A dangerous cycle that could have ended my life at any point. This is what my body was horribly addicted to, like a heroin addict. I could not break the cycles with my conscious mind. I had to go deep into my subconscious mind and heal the deep inner wounds from childhood, the ones that I ran away from all my life. It wasn't until I healed these wounds and I stopped running away from my fears when everything changed. I processed the pain and I changed the false-beliefs I had about myself. Through visualization, I was finally able to break free from the trauma-bonding I had battled with. I was finally able to move forward into my new life, full of peace, love and joy. Find what works best for you in order to heal and thrive!

CHAPTER 7

You are the Most Important Person

You are the foundation of your life. If your foundation is weak, anything you build on it will fall apart at some point or another. In order to reach self-actualization, you need to build on a solid foundation. By focusing on yourself and not the other person, you have control over what you can change, which is yourself. According to Maslow's hierarchy of needs. The first base or foundation is having your basic physiological needs met. For example, air, water, food, shelter, sleep, clothing and reproduction. The second level of the triangle is safety needs. You can not build to the next level until you have achieved the first level. The second level includes personal security, sources of income, employment, resources, health, and property. The third level of this triangle you build upon, is love and sense of belonging. This includes friendships, intimacy, family, sense of connection, are all vital parts of the third level. The fourth level is self-esteem needs. You need respect, self-esteem, status, recognition, strength and freedom. Once you reach this fourth level, you can finally climb to self-actualization, which is at the top of the pyramid. This is the desire to become the most that you can be, when you start living your dream. This is the goal and destination. Once you arrive you are thriving and living your best life!!! To reach this peak, all the previous levels have to be met.

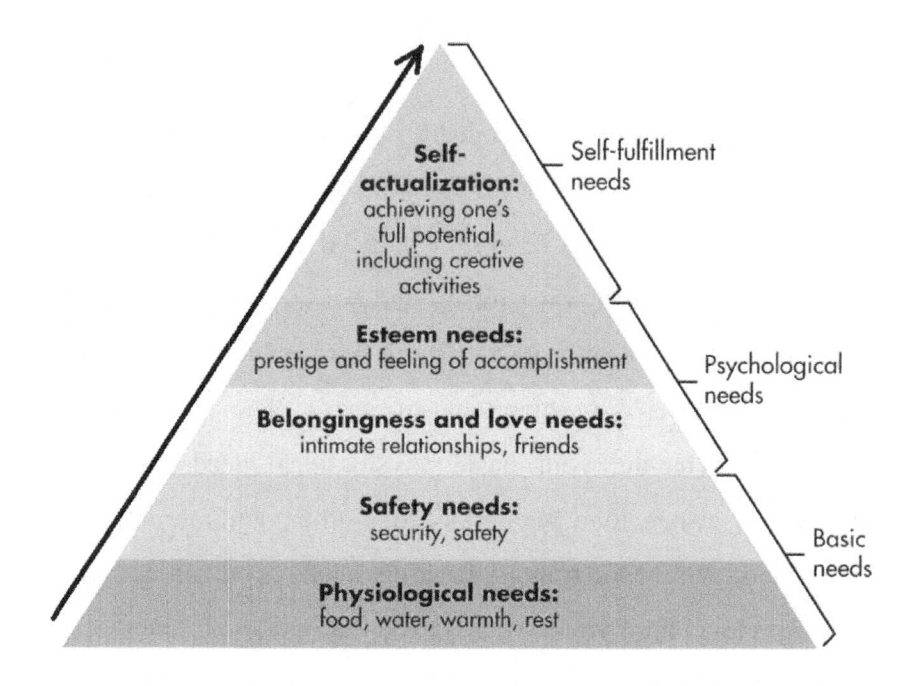

Self-actualization: achieving one's full potential, including creative activities — Self-fulfillment needs

Esteem needs: prestige and feeling of accomplishment

Belongingness and love needs: intimate relationships, friends

— Psychological needs

Safety needs: security, safety

Physiological needs: food, water, warmth, rest

— Basic needs

More importantly, we need to clear our paradigms of self-doubt, fear and negative thoughts about ourselves. I want us to focus on the fourth step because it is so critical in order to reach the top level.

In order to have self-esteem, and freedom, you need to focus on yourself. You cannot control, fix or change anyone else. The work has to be done on the inside of you. Going inward to see what you need to work on in order to change your inner identity. Perhaps your parents called you names and placed beliefs in your mind that you would never amount to anything. Maybe your parents didn't praise you or tell you that you were smart or beautiful. The lack of love and affirmation, told you the story you believed. You believed you were not pretty, smart or that you were not going to accomplish your goals or dreams. Those are crushing words to a child who takes them to heart and creates a poor self-image. You want to build your self-esteem and inner strength. You need to get to a point where you truly and honestly believe in your heart of hearts that you are smart and have a grand purpose in life. In order to heal your inner wounds, you want to forgive yourself and any guilt or shame you feel about your past. If you look closely, these feelings of guilt or shame do not belong to you. They belong to the abuser. As you heal, you will have an urge to go back and get an apology or restitution from him or her, but let it go. Rising above it will elevate you even higher and you will heal even more. Don't waste your energy. In cases, where there is current violence and emotional abuse, you want to call the police, file a report and press charges. If you go this route, make sure you write down dates, times and take photos of every episode that occurs so you will have proof in court. Sadly, psychological abuse is so hard to prove. However, in England and Wales, it is now a law that is enforced with a penalty of up to 5 years in prison. Even then, abusers hardly ever change. Instead, you want to focus your energy on your own healing, personal needs and desires. Think about who you were before you met him or her. What were your passions? What did you enjoy doing? What brought you joy? You have to start making the change within yourself in order to move from surviving to thriving. You cannot give to others what you do not have. If you want to be happy, you need to place yourself in a more vibrant and positive state of mind. You cannot give love and joy to anyone if you do not have it in your own heart. You should not depend on people or things to have peace and love. You want to focus on your energy and no one else's. Your foundation has to be strong. Then and only then will you be able to give from your abundance. So how do you do that? One of the best ways to change your energy and your state of mind is to raise your vibrations.

Raising Your Vibrations

What do I mean by that? The concept was very foreign to me when I first heard it. At first, I thought it was crazy talk. According to Dr. David Hawkins, M.D., PH.D., in his widely-known Map of Consciousness, he presents a diagram of the vibrational frequency of its corresponding emotion. Your vibration is actually your energy vibrating at a certain frequency. Every cell in our body from the top of our head to the tip of our toes, is made of vibrational energy. He further states 99% of the world's population lives at a frequency

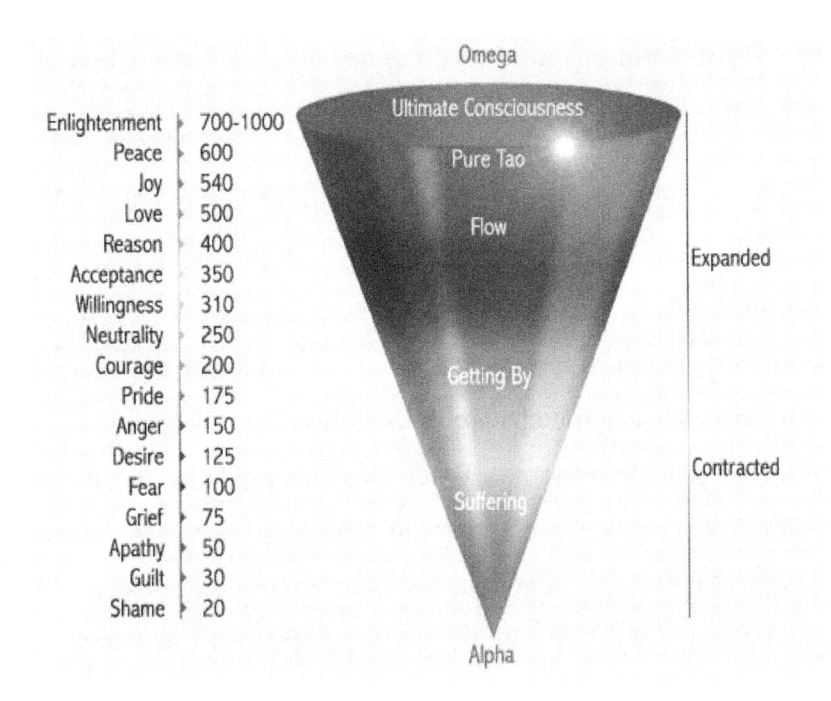

Enlightenment	700-1000	
Peace	600	
Joy	540	
Love	500	
Reason	400	
Acceptance	350	Expanded
Willingness	310	
Neutrality	250	
Courage	200	
Pride	175	
Anger	150	
Desire	125	
Fear	100	Contracted
Grief	75	
Apathy	50	
Guilt	30	
Shame	20	

Omega — Ultimate Consciousness — Pure Tao — Flow — Getting By — Suffering — Alpha

Below 200!! This equates to just getting by. The emotions at really low frequencies are anger, fear, guilt and shame. Individuals rarely live their best life from these frequencies. The challenge is to raise our vibrations between 700 - 1000 or to obtain peace and love. When you become aware, you can feel the vibration of others. Knowledge is key to your happiness and vitality. Vibrations do not lie. Pay close attention when you meet someone for the first time. What does their energy tell you about them? Pay close attention, even if they smile from ear to ear, how do you feel in their presence? Your body can literally reject someone's energy and your anxiety will start acting up any time negative energy disrupts your spirit. Listen to your body and what it tells you about other's energy. How do you feel around the people in your life today? Can you feel their vibe? Recall from chapter 3, vibrations attract similar vibrations; low vibrations attract more low vibrations.

For example, if you live in fear or afraid of falling, guess what? You will fall because you're attracting it. Your thoughts put out messages to the universe and the universe sends back to you what you are putting out. It is a law of the universe, the law of attraction, like gravity. We can not change it. Even if you don't believe it, you will attract what you vibrate. When two energies meet in different vibrations, they cancel each other out. When a positive vibe meets a low vibe it equals no vibe or a flat line. Therefore, when you are around people with low vibrations, their energy will squash yours. Your energy is depleted and you feel drained. This is how you feel around toxic people. You can keep increasing your vibration, but then you lose it around them. Life is energy. If your energy keeps getting canceled, guess what? You are threatening your vitality and health. This is why you don't want to remain with toxic people for long periods of time. You need good energy for your body and mind, just like food, water and sleep. Toxic people will keep depleting your body's energetic resources and you will slowly start to get sick. Your energy is what narcissists thrive on. However, if you raise your vibrations, you can slow down aging. Have you known people who are older yet look very young? The reason for this is they have high vibrations. They are very youthful in appearance but also in mind and spirit. You can change your life if you change your vibration. This is the secret of the fountain of youth.

This has been scientifically proven in the works of Dr. Bruce H. Lipton PhD in his book Biology of Belief. As we reviewed earlier, our cells have little antennae that pick up vibrations around us and react accordingly. There are many ways to raise your vibrations. Here are just a few and where to find more information:

- LOVE - is the highest vibration of all, love yourself the most
- Breathing techniques - Deep breathing - Three Point Breath as explained in Chapter 1
- Breath of Fire - Fast and quick breaths while ten fingers are touching for 30 seconds - YouTube for examples
- The healing sounds like Ra Ma Da Sa - YouTube - play for a while
- Healing vibrations like Hertz 432, 417, 528, 639, 963, - Clearing your negative energy, calm down anxiety, stop overthinking - YouTube and play for a while
- Calming meditations - sounds of the ocean - sounds of the woods - YouTube or google
- Foods - diet made of plant based, natural, organic are best, powerful plants
- Nature - Surround yourself in nature. Nature has high vibrations - walking, hiking, running, swimming
- Being around water - ocean side, lakes, rivers, waterfalls have very high vibrations

- Mantras - Tina Turner's favorite - many different kinds to clear Chakras - YouTube or google

- Guided Meditation - for all issues - I like Bob Proctor's on stress and money - Google or YouTube

- Prayer - Faith in Higher Power - belief without any doubt even though circumstances are different

- Reiki - healing vibration - look for local practitioners, for my friends in Phoenix, AZ check out www.sozohealinghouse.com/

- Harmonium - Transcendental healing that addresses the innate relationship of the body and mind - look for local practitioners - recommend Bird Mejia @ www.sozohealinghouse.com/

- Magnet Therapy - Works well for health and emotional issues - look for local practitioners - recommend Claudia Rubio at www.sozohealinghouse.com/

- EMDR - if you feel like you need more support and professional assistance look for local practitioners

- Affirmations - repeating your affirmations verbally and in writing - "I love and accept myself just the way I am" "I am beautiful" "I am enough" "I am strong"

- Mirror work - telling yourself you love yourself. Love and accept your body aloud as well while in front of the mirror

- Visualization - Close your eyes and imagine yourself on your favorite place on earth. See yourself living the life you want, feel it with your body and soul. Know you can accomplish anything you set your mind to do, believe in yourself!!

One of my favorites that I practice daily is the three point breath. You inhale for a count of four seconds. You hold your breath for a count of four seconds. Exhale for a count of four seconds. You can increase the seconds as time goes on. Repeating the breath work at least three times a day approximately five minutes in duration up to 15 minutes helps to increase your vibrations. Have you ever noticed your breathing when you are feeling stressed? Take note, next time you are stressed. The breathing is very shallow and short. You are not getting enough oxygen into your lungs, brain or body. Raising your vibrations is very important to change the low vibrations to high vibrations and change your life.

My second favorite method to accomplish this goal is being in nature. Nature has such high vibrations. I love spending time outdoors hiking, running or just walking around a lake. Spending time outside for 20 minutes a day can increase your vibrations significantly. If all you do is walk your dog or just take a stroll in your neighborhood is all you need. Notice the abundance of life around you while you walk. From the birds in the sky to the busy ants beneath you. Like King Solomon said, they don't stress about how they will eat tomorrow. They live in the moment and enjoy life, we can learn alot from them.

Certain sounds have high vibrations. There are many different types of sounds that you can listen to. I listen to Hertz 432 if I have problems falling asleep. It really helps me to fall asleep quickly and rest with more peace. I also play it during the day when I need to increase my vibrations due to feeling melancholy. Music has good vibrations as well depending on the music you listen to. It is very important to listen to the lyrics and decipher what type of vibration the song or music is putting out. You want to ensure you're always listening to music with high vibrations.

Writing affirmations in the morning helps increase your vibrations as well. Repeat them to yourself throughout the day. Write them in the present tense, "I am so happy and grateful now that...." I used to write them on sticky notes and place them on my mirror where I could read them every morning. I read them to myself over and over as I was getting ready for work. I also did the mirror while getting ready for my day or any time I needed to. While at work, I would sometimes go to the bathroom and do mirror work if I was feeling down or emotional for whatever reason. A lot of times I could not pinpoint why I was feeling sad, but just doing the mirror work and the breath work significantly changed my vibrations. You can not help or protect your loved ones if you are not strong or taking care of yourself.

Visualization is one of the most effective ways to increase your vibrations. If I feel anxious, I see myself on my favorite place on earth, the ocean. I have an island I go to where I sunbathe. I observe the colors of the sky and feel the sand beneath my toes. I hear the sound of the birds in the sky and the ocean waves. I let sunlight into my body from top of my head to the bottom of my toes. Another powerful visualization is to imagine yourself in your future state, seeing yourself how you want to live. See yourself living your dreams and hold the thought. Act as if you are already living in that state. Be grateful for the blessings as if you already received them. It works miracles when you live in this manner. I can help you live the life you want. These are some of my favorite ways to raise my vibrations.

Self-Partnering and Self-Love

What do I mean by self-partnering? The love for yourself should be greater than the love for anyone or anything else on earth. It means when you feel sad or down, you don't run away from yourself or your inner child. Especially when your inner child is crying out to you during a trigger. How do you know when your child is crying? Listen to your feelings, stop and journal when you are mad, sad, anxious, or feeling down. You want to parent yourself like a parent does to a child. Whenever your child is crying, you run to the child, pick him/her up to see what's wrong? You want to know why he or she is crying or if he or she is hurt? You then cradle the child and put a band-aid where they hurt themselves or do whatever it takes to make them feel better. This is especially important to make yourself whole by loving yourself, taking care of yourself and supplying all of the love you need for yourself. A lot of us expect a person or an external source to make us happy. We tell ourselves, "When I get a promotion or a new car then I will be happy. Once I find the perfect man or woman, then I will be happy." Happiness is achieved in the moment, we make the choice. When we love ourselves, our happiness flows from the inside out. Our partner will reflect the love we have for ourselves.

It's important not to run away from yourself when you're feeling sad or angry. Doing the mirror work we reviewed earlier by looking into your eyes and telling yourself, "(Your Name) I love you. I really really love you. You are the love of your life and I will never leave you. I will always honor, cherish, and respect you all the days of my life." Repeat it over and over until you feel better. The repetition helps to engrave it into your subconscious mind.

No More Self-Sabotage

What do I mean by self-sabotage? This happens when we actively or passively prevent ourselves from reaching our goals. Weight loss, career or relationships are but a few of these goals. Some of the reasons we engage in this behavior are lack of self-worth, fear of success or failure. We talk negatively to ourselves thereby reducing our self-esteem and belief in ourselves. We tell ourselves, "Why even try if I know I will not lose the weight or get the promotion?" These thoughts stem from our sub consciousness and increase self-doubt and fears of rejection. It also includes procrastination, self-medicating with drugs or alcohol, or comfort eating. If you are not sure if you are self-sabotaging, ask yourself the following questions: Am I avoiding what needs to be done? Am I always procrastinating? Am I prioritizing instant gratification? Am I not prioritizing self-care? Am I focusing on self-defeating thoughts? If you answered yes to any of the previous questions, you might be self-sabotaging. Consider what is preventing you from obtaining what you want? Get really real and raw with your answers. If you are afraid of failure, focus on building your self-confidence by bringing to memory all the times you did achieve success. Change the negative thought with a positive one. Then imagine yourself achieving your new goal and create an action plan to help you get there. If you can hold an image in your mind, you can hold it in your hand. Your goal will become a reality. Changing your old paradigm and beliefs about yourself will make self-sabotage a thing of the past. Focus on self-care and positive thinking. I know when I am stressed or anxious, I crave junk food. I have to find healthier ways to release my stress instead. The first step is awareness of this behavior and identify better ways to cope. For example, instead of eating junk food, take the dog or kids for a walk. You can take a hot shower or do something you love like painting or playing a game. Make a list of your favorite things to do and cross the list off little by little. Stop running away from yourself. If you feel like crying, then cry. Let the tears roll down your cheeks, there is healing in tears. If you want to scream then scream until you let it all out. If you want to break something, break an old dish or jar, just make sure you are doing it safely so as not to harm others or yourself. Once you get it all out, take a deep breath, step back and take time to understand what caused the emotion and make sure you heal it. It is ok to express yourself in a positive productive way. You should get it out of your body. I have done all of the above mentioned things to express myself. Now when I am stressed, I go for a run or workout at home or gym (before COVID 19). I find ways everyday to take care of myself by reducing stress levels and anxiety. I now believe in myself and focus on having a positive mindset. You can do anything I can do!

Be Kind to Yourself

Instead of stinking thinking, focus on treating yourself kindly, find the things that you love or once loved. I know it's hard at first if you abandoned your passions a long time ago. Think about what your passions were as a child. What did you enjoy doing? How did you spend your free time when you were not in school or working? Some of these can include running, sports, riding a bike, playing games, drawing, playing an instrument, walking to a friends house or painting. Make time to take care of yourself by spending anywhere from 15 minutes to an hour, or however long you need to feel better. You can also pamper yourself with a massage, pedicure, manicure, even if you do them at home. Men should take care of themselves as well by taking hikes, journaling, reading up on things you want to learn more about are all ways of self care.

Focus on things that make you physically and emotionally feel better. Creativity can flow doing the things you love. Be patient with yourself and do not talk negatively or say mean things to yourself. It takes a lot of effort and awareness to catch your thoughts in order to change them. When you start thinking negative thoughts just stop and drop the thought. Literally physically visualize you dropping the thought and thinking of something positive instead. Go back to your affirmations. If you wrote them down on your phone or on your sticky note, go back and read them to yourself. Repeat affirmations all day long until you notice your thoughts turning positive automatically. Focus on your vision, the more you do this, the closer you bring it to you. Here is a good affirmation from Louise House. "I love and approve of myself exactly as I am. I love and approve of myself exactly as I am. I love and approve of myself exactly as I am." Repeat it over and over to change your thought patterns and subconscious mind.

What Are You Willing to Let Go?

Are you willing to let go of fear of rejection, criticism, retaliation, loneliness, and void of passion? None of these things bring you joy, peace or love. These states are all low vibrational frequencies. Once you let go of these things, you will experience and accept love and good vibrations. You will embrace yourself for who you truly are.

You are the most important person, that's who you are. If you love and support yourself, so will others. Other people will mirror the love you have for yourself. If you love yourself deeply, you will attract a partner who loves you deeply. If you take care of yourself, your partner and family will do the same.

You and your faith on what is not seen, is your foundation and your rock. Make a strong foundation and build upon it. In order to thrive, you have to be who you really are and not who others want you to be. Do not worry about the expectations of society, work, family, church, culture or your own expectations. Be you and embrace who you are just as you are. For me, once I realized how important it was to stop focusing on other people and to start focusing on me, my life turned around. I was the most important person and I needed to take care of myself. No one else was taking care of me. Another life coach, Robin Minor, helped me to understand the importance of getting to know me and self-care. This was an important piece of the puzzle. I needed to know who I was, what I loved to do and what made me happy. I had lost myself in others. I didn't know who I was anymore and I didn't know what I wanted. I didn't know what my likes and dislikes were. Once I spent time thinking about the things I liked, I started to do the things I enjoyed. I started taking good care of myself, like taking bubble baths and getting massages. I bought myself clothes that I liked and treated myself with love and respect. I learned to increase my vibrations through breathing techniques, listening to healing sounds and affirming how much I loved and accepted myself just the way I was. I started to build a strong vibration and felt better by focusing on me.

In this state, however, I still kept going back to my ex-husband. It wasn't until I healed the trauma-bond that I was able to go NO CONTACT. I was able to settle the divorce without a lot of anxiety or stress to ensure equitable division of debts and assets. We acquired over 100K in debts after he quit his job without a good reason. He wanted to take all the assets without paying the debts that were all in my name. I can not impress on you how supercritical it is to break any and all trauma-bonds in your body. Once you do this, you start loving and focusing on yourself. Building a strong foundation, you will start to see how your world begins to change for the better. Everything will start falling into place and you will feel peace.

CHAPTER 8

Finding Your Power, Your Voice and Speaking Your Truth

Your real authentic self will become more evident as you do the work to heal your inner wounds. As you start loving and accepting who you really are, you will become more empowered. Once you start doing the things you love, your life will take a turn for the best. Taking your power back is first accomplished by focusing on your emotions and needs, instead of giving away your energy and attention to others. Staying in your power means nothing anyone says or does will affect you in a negative way. It means you remain in control of your emotions and do not react to toxic people. Toxic people just want to get a reaction from you to satisfy their ego. They press on your unhealed wounds from childhood. They will make fun of you, belittle and make you feel awkward and insignificant in order to make themselves feel better. You are in your power when you can step away and grow yourself up from a trigger. When you do not react out of anger or emotions but instead, you turn inwards to nurture yourself. I love this quote, "Without exception, every breakdown harolds a breakthrough of equal magnitude," from an unknown author. Your pain can be transported to power. A power so great that you can change the trajectory of your life to a meaningful and purpose driven way of living. Living in your power, can bring a narcissist to justice, when your triggers no longer control your actions. Bringing the narcissist to justice is as simple as healing yourself. You will not give them any more energy at all. Cut toxic people and situations out of your life in order to avoid triggers, feelings of insecurity, toxic shame and feelings of abandonment. What is toxic shame? According to De Cannonville, "it cuts deep into the core of oneself. It inhibits the mind in a way that makes the person feel chronically inadequate, deficient and faulty. It is embedded in the invisible subconscious mind and casts a shadow, restricting personal greatness."

Finding Your Voice

When you find yourself in your power, you will find your voice. In Christine De Canonville's book, When Shame Begets Shame, "The memory of trauma rather than being processed through the brain and moving to long term memory, it ricochets and becomes lodged within the cells of the body." For me, as it was for her, it became trapped in my throat. Thinking about it makes my throat start to throb. During trauma, the victim may experience a term called Freeze Fright. This happens during the terror when a victim becomes trauma-bonded with the aggressor as a means to survive. He or she is torn between fight or flight. On one hand, he or she knows what will happen if they fight. In response he or she may become compliant, obedient and submissive in order to avoid the ramifications of going against the aggressor. This renders the victim unable to leave or fight back, thereby "freezing."

For years after, I would have terrifying nightmares where I would try to scream at the top of my lungs, but nothing would come out, not a beep. I kept quiet of everything that happened to me until long after I realized what had happened. Even after I told a few people, I bottled it up again. I went to counseling, but I never expressed the anger and frustration I had inside. I didn't release the anger or pain. I pretended that everything was fine. I continued to feel trapped until I did the work and faced my fears and pain. Now I am writing this book to help others out of pain, shame and feelings of powerlessness.

You should know the world needs to hear your voice. Your voice is alive and your voice matters. Your voice and experiences can help other people who are where you have been. You have an important message and just sharing your story can give hope and strength to other people. I had drowned my voice so deep that I could not hear myself. I turned from my truth and pretended to live another life. I almost didn't break my silence but I knew God had a different purpose for my life than I had for myself. I now embrace my past because it has made me who I am today. There are so many women, children and men living with so much pain, guilt and shame. I want you to know it was not your fault. You did not cause it. You did not create it and you should not be ashamed. You should not live in fear and isolation. Your life should not suffer because of the actions of evil people who inflicted pain in your life. In due time, they will be accountable to all the evil they committed.

Speaking Your Truth

When finding your voice and your power, you will be able to speak YOUR truth. Expressing your feelings and how it affected you is an important step in the healing process. Through speaking your truth, you begin to break the chains that have held you down for so long. Your platform can be anything you want it to be. As a parent, talking to your children about your past struggles can really open their eyes and help them stay safe and away from people who want to harm them. Breaking the silence stops the perpetrators from continuing to work in the darkness. By shedding light on the truth, you bring awareness and teach others how to avoid falling prey. You take the power away from the evil ones and empower the people you come into contact with. Wherever you are planted in life, you can make an impact on those around you. As teachers, doctors, mothers, sisters, brothers, friends, entertainers, you have a voice to help others. Talking about it helps give courage to those living in fear. It gives a voice to the voiceless who can not stand up for themselves. This book is dedicated to all those women and children who are voiceless. You should know that the shame is not yours, it belongs to the abuser. Know you are blameless, no matter how guilty you may feel. Forgiving yourself is also a vital step in this process. You did what you needed to do in order to survive. You are resilient, strong, resourceful, full of ingenuity and inner strength!

Who Are You?

Coming out of a long-term abusive relationship, we may be left wondering who we are. When we take our masks, labels and other hats we wear off, we begin to understand who we really are. Who are you without the mom, sister, wife, brother, husband, or career hat? You're an intelligent, strong, powerful, human being that can accomplish anything you set your mind to do. This is who you are. Focus on your deep inner desires or core beliefs without anyone else's inputs. Ask yourself, what are my strengths? What am I good at? What do I enjoy doing? What are my passions? Your purpose lies in one of these answers if not all. Many of these we don't value like compassion, empathy or love. When you find yourself, you find your purpose and your voice will become stronger. These are the most precious gifts we have to offer to this world. When you understand who you truly are, you can understand who you are truly meant to be. Your power and genius becomes unleashed.

You can start by exploring your creative side. This can take many forms like painting, crocheting, playing an instrument, dancing, singing, or learning something you always wanted to learn. I began to paint, I love art. I always wanted to paint with acrylics, but I never gave myself permission or time to do this. I never gave myself permission to do any of the things that I wanted because I was not allowed as a child. I wasn't allowed to play and have fun. As the eldest, I had to be perfect. I had to be a perfect role model to my siblings. If I wasn't, then I was punished. I never enjoyed being a child. I grew up too fast and was responsible for everyone else's actions. My paradigm belief was if I had too much fun then something bad would happen to me. Through my thoughts, bad things did happen which kept reinforcing this belief. It kept becoming a reality because of the law of attraction we talked about earlier. Now as an adult, I give myself permission to have fun, to laugh and to enjoy life. What are your passions and dreams? What did you enjoy doing as a child? What did you want to be when you grew up? I keep bringing this question up because there is hidden treasure in the answers. Take your time and ponder on what made you happy as a child. A lot of times we become who our caregivers, church, society, educational system says we should become. We adapt to the norms we were raised in, while denying our inner hopes and dreams.

Begin by making a list and prioritize them by what brings you the most peace and joy. Next, put a date by when you will complete the items. Without a date, it is again a dream. You want to create a timeline so you have something to work towards. It is these things that you love, who you truly are and your true passions in life. Wouldn't it be wonderful if you could make a living doing the things you love? It would not be work would it? I firmly believe when you do the things you love, the money will follow. As you begin to elevate yourself and move your energy upward, you will also become more confident. Your current friends may or may not rise with you. Be ready to lose some of these relationships, who do not share your new goals or vibrations in your new life.

New Relationships

During this time of transition, as you stop accepting toxicity in your life, people will come and go. Embrace the new people coming into your life who are energetically more vibrant than the old ones. There is a saying that goes, 'show me who your friends are and I will show you who you are.' If you think about your closest friends and their lives, this is the level you will reach. Strive to be with people who carry positive vibes and great energy. They will bring you up versus taking you down. When you embrace your new life and your new heart, you will be free to take off and fly. Your new path in life has changed forever and for the better. Be ready to have old friendships evaporate. Make room for new relationships and new people in your life.

For me, once I knew I had enough, I was determined to improve the quality of my life. I wanted to be happy, smile and laugh. My first vision board was my guide and kept reminding me of my goal. It had nothing with material things, it was about a state of being happy, full of joy and laughter. That's how I envisioned living my life and what it is today! I had to take off all my masks and start being the real me. I had to face my character defects and stop running away from my pain. Facing my pain has been the hardest, scariest, most difficult thing I have ever done. I was able to release the pain in order to heal and move forward. As Melanie Evans says "We can not heal what we are not ready to feel." I followed my body in order to bring out the false beliefs and pain that had been stored in my subconscious mind. At this stage, I had healed a lot but I still had a lot of work to do. However, I was building on a strong foundation.

CHAPTER 9

Exiting Toxic Relationships

I purposely left this chapter towards the end, because in order for you to exit toxic relationships, your foundation and your belief in yourself has to be strong. You must fall in love with yourself by doing the work in the previous chapters. To strengthen yourself enough to find the courage to leave is critical. After years of depending on this person, people or lifestyle, leaving it behind is the most difficult thing to do. You can not expect someone else to love you more than you love yourself. Love or lack of love will show up in your partner like looking in the mirror. You cannot love the other person more than you love yourself. Loving and self-partnering with yourself throughout this process is key. Focus on the reality, facts and truths. Taking the toxic person out of the equation is liberating for your life. Understand and accept you cannot change them. If they wanted to change then they would have already done so. Actions speak louder than words. Once you heal and love yourself, you can stop accepting what you don't deserve.

Stop Accepting What You Don't Deserve

If someone does not bring you joy, peace or happiness, ask yourself why are they in your life? You do not have to accept less than what you deserve, no matter who it is. If someone does not respect you, you do not owe them anything. Respect starts by respecting yourself. By allowing others to disrespect you, you are not respecting yourself. Look at toxic people and energy vampires as teachers that came to teach you something very important. What did they come to teach? They came to teach us that we still have work to do within ourselves. We still had traumas and wounds that we had to heal in order to thrive and be the best versions of ourselves we can possibly be. If you're unsure if the person you are with is toxic or not, think about their energy and how you feel around their presence. Listen to your body. What does your gut tell you? What do their actions tell you? How does someone demonstrate true love? Is lying and cheating true love?

Listen to Your Body

Your body tells you everything you need to know. Do you trust it? If not, why not? You want to get to a point where you trust yourself 100%. I know during narcissistic abuse, you question your stability, sanity and trust in yourself. Owning your gut instincts is loving yourself. Your body knows what it feels and what is good for you. Follow what your body tells you. Do you feel stress, anxiety, or fearful around this person? Do you feel inadequate? What feelings come over you when you think about this person? Listen to your gut and don't make excuses for the other person. Don't excuse their behavior as love, protection or concern. Go with your first initial gut instinct. It is always right. Don't forget the vicious cycle:

honeymoon, build-up, blow-up and make-up. Be honest with yourself. Your vitality, health, and happiness depends on it. Abusive relationships end in one of three ways. One, the abuser ends up taking the life of the victim. Two, the victim ends up in a psychiatric ward with an emotional breakdown and on medication to regulate emotions. Three, the victim ends up taking his or her life. None of these are good outcomes. Get out while you still have your health and mind intact!

Let Go of Control

Let go of trying to control others. You will not win arguments with toxic people. They drain your energy and your life. I tried to control my environment and people in my life. However, I was the one that ended up being controlled. I handed my power away and my sense of self. When you give up control and focus only on the things you can control, it changes the game. I wanted people to change to my satisfaction and I didn't accept them as they were. When I saw them for who they really were, it made me realize what I was and wasn't willing to accept. I put boundaries in place and they did not like them. Boundaries keep us safe from being taken advantage of. You have a right to say no to anything you do not want to do, including sex, even if you are married. Do not allow someone to guilt you for not wanting to have sex or do anything you do not want to do. No means no. Hold your boundaries firm and if they do not respect your boundaries then they are disrespecting you.

Future Generations

When you heal, you heal seven generations before and after you. Your children and the children you reach learn by watching you. Many parents stay in toxic relationships for their kids. They think that they're doing the best thing for the children by staying. The reality is the children receive more harm than good. Remember, they are absorbing everything they see and creating subconscious patterns up to age 6. Do you want them to repeat your story? Do you want your grandchildren repeating the cycles of abuse and their children? Statistics of child abuse from NAASA.org, show about 30 percent of abused and neglected children will later abuse their own children, continuing the horrible cycle of abuse. About 80% of 21 year olds that were abused as children met criteria for at least one psychological disorder (NAACC 2011) Link.

It further states 1 in 4 girls and 1 in 6 boys will be sexually molested by the time they are 18 years old. About 25% of the population has abuse in their background. This is about 81 million people living in the United States of America. I believe the number is higher due to all the unreported abuse that occurs, especially in boys. I have met hundreds of women that have been abused. Your children are better off in a safe environment, away from toxic people and shame. They will thank you for it.

Remember epigenetics? What are your children learning from you? You're teaching them that it is OK to be verbally, mentally and/or physically abused. You are showing them the movie of how their future lives will be. You will cement in their subconscious patterns what will dictate their future. Is that what you really want for your children? I don't think that's the case. If anything, heal yourself for their future, they're better off in a positive and vibrant environment where they can learn self-esteem and thrive. Your kids don't choose the family they're born into. However, you can choose the environment they live in. Changing your future also changes your children's future and your grandchildren's future. In order to start the process, you have to let go of victimization. You're not a victim any longer. Not only are you a survivor, but you are a thriver. Start seeing and believing this into your life. Remember, the vibrations you put out is what you will get back, so within, so without.

Once you leave, if you can, go no contact or modify the contact. The feelings and urges you have to reach out will pass. With every passing day, week, month and year, the feelings will subside. When you go inwards and heal your inner wounds, it makes it so much easier and your recovery so much faster. When you don't heal your inner wounds, you can, even after you leave, stay stuck, even if it's just in your mind. You may find yourself going back and giving your energy to the person who abused you. You can meet another similar person and continue to be trapped in a vicious cycle, unable to move forward in life. Unable to achieve happiness or live to your full potential. If you don't leave, you can continue the vicious cycles.

You will risk everything: your health, your kids, your home and everything you know about yourself. Disease will creep in, as many victims develop rare diseases and common illnesses like cancer, heart attacks, auto-immune diseases, thyroid disorder, high blood pressure, anxiety, gut issues, and the list goes on and on.

The effects of these illnesses can linger, long after you have left the person or abusive situation. It is very important to heal and let go of the shame and guilt that was passed on to you during the abuse. There is a difference between toxic shame and healthy shame. Understanding your false-beliefs are not true, can give you freedom to be your true self. Join support groups to help you come out of isolation. I have an online support group at SeleneFBgroup. There are many support groups locally you can google like codependents anonymous. You can also find helpful videos on YouTube, Facebook, Instagram and other online resources. You can also sign up for my online coaching program to help you through the steps described in this book at www.selenelifecoach.com. Remember, you are not alone, there is plenty of support but you have to reach out.

Forgive Yourself

Do not feel bad or guilty for the decisions you made. You did the best you could given the circumstances. I believe your past has made you who are today. Survivors of trauma and abuse are real silent heroes. You should be given a medal for your bravery. Be your own hero! I send you all my love for showing up for yourself. A lot of people don't make it or become the aggressors themselves. You overcame the worst situations and came through triumphantly. You have started and continue your healing journey by reading this book. I congratulate you and receive praise from me as well for making it this far. No matter where you are in your journey, know that you are strong, resilient, compassionate and caring. You deserve to be free of any shame or guilt. On the contrary, turn the toxic shame and guilt into ammunition to continue to heal and reach all of your goals and dreams. Create goals that scare you, think way above what you think you can accomplish! If you can think it, you can do it!

Grief

Grief is a necessary part of the process of leaving a narcissist. The different stages include denial, anger, bargaining, depression and acceptance.

Kübler-Ross Grief Cycle

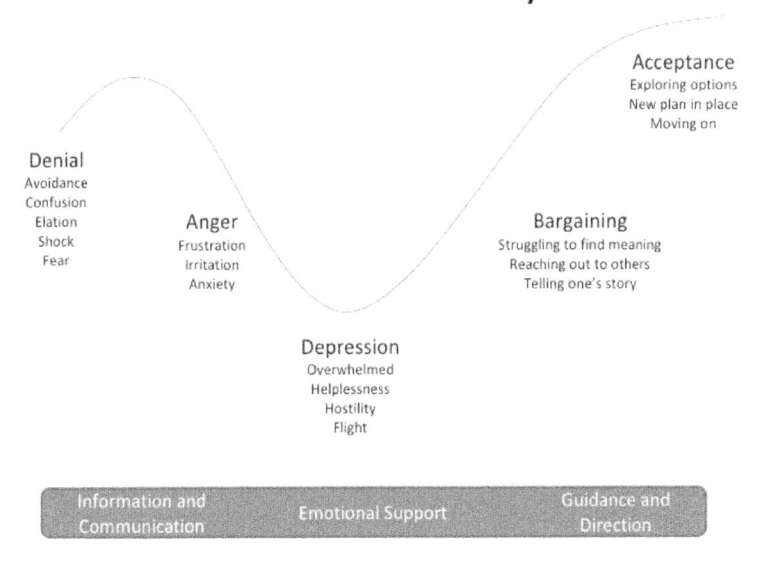

Denial
Avoidance
Confusion
Elation
Shock
Fear

Anger
Frustration
Irritation
Anxiety

Depression
Overwhelmed
Helplessness
Hostility
Flight

Bargaining
Struggling to find meaning
Reaching out to others
Telling one's story

Acceptance
Exploring options
New plan in place
Moving on

| Information and Communication | Emotional Support | Guidance and Direction |

Be prepared to go through this process. Let the pain and anger out by journaling and talking about it. Talk about it in your support groups. Unprocessed grief blocks the heart. By not dealing, it can lead to emotional numbness, depression, anger and addictions. You want to be open and clear to receive your new life by removing all the blocks. Securing accountability partners can help you stay on track. Coaches and mentors help to call you out when you are going into denial or if they see old patterns surface. Surround yourself with a good support system. Know healing is a process and it doesn't happen overnight. It is not a one time event either. Once you start to heal, there are different levels of healing. You will find that the deeper you go, the more you will find. However, the rewards outweigh the temporary discomfort. You will start feeling better each time and getting stronger. You are liberating yourself from all the guilt and shame you acquired over the years, those untrue beliefs about yourself. Breaking the chains of bondage will allow you to fly and be your true self in order to thrive in life. Understand these toxic people came to serve a purpose. They came to show us what we needed to heal. After you reach a certain level, know you may still have unhealed wounds. The process is a lifelong journey.

The sooner you start your healing journey, the sooner you will feel better and end the cycles. Don't wait for another bad relationship or situation to bring you back to this place. If you keep coming across narcissists, know that you still have unhealed wounds because these people continue to show up in your life. Healing the trauma-bonds will allow you to heal and thrive. When you walk away, know you have healed enough to have the courage to leave.

For me, once I understood how I got to where I was and where I wanted to go, the rest became history. I understood the need to create boundaries around the things that did not bring me peace, joy or happiness. One of the hardest things I had to let go of was my fairy tale family. I had to face reality and let it go. I was giving and giving and receiving nothing in return. I was enabling people to be irresponsible and disrespectful towards me. I was disregarded and used for my resources. I was not loved because I did not love myself.

I felt trapped and unable to change my situation for fear of what people would say. I felt so much shame and guilt, I blamed myself. I could not bring myself to talk to anyone about my problems. No one knew the pain I suffered in silence. I started to have mini breakdowns and I could barely make it through one day. All of my energy and financial resources were being sucked out of me slowly that I did not realize it. Like a lobster in boiling water. It just sits in the pot thinking everything is ok, while the temperature rises, it doesn't realize it's being boiled. My situation was getting worse. I had to get out or I would lose my mind for good. My adrenals were in overhaul drive day and night. I had no peace and I avoided going to my own home I purchased with my own hard-earned money.

Until one day, someone saw me and offered her hand to help me. Thank you, Robin Minor. She was a key to the changes I needed to make and gave me the courage to do what I needed to do for me, for my sanity and well-being. I had to feel safe first and foremost. After a year, I went no contact to end the trauma-bonding once and for all. It had kept me in that vicious cycle. It was so hard at first and I kept breaking no contact over and over. Every time I went back, I received more pain and abuse. It kept me even more trauma-bonded than before. He would sprinkle nice things in between to keep me engaged and confused. I still couldn't accept the hard truth and I kept hoping he would change. I didn't understand the concept at first or why I kept going back for more. Until I understood narcissists and trauma-bonding. I immediately started the work of visualization and releasing the trauma that was trapped in my body. I was finally able to come out feeling strong. Soon after, I finally maintained no contact. He tried hovering me back in but I blocked him out of everything: email, social media, my phone, work emails, everything. I didn't know all the ways I could block him until I did it. I asked my family not to relay his messages to me. I would not allow any more trauma to come into my life.

I was finally able to stop the addiction and come off the trauma-bond drug. Although at first I felt like I was going to literally die. However, the simple visualization process of healing the thriver using quantum tools made the difference in my life in order to break free once and for all. Are you willing to do what it takes to heal and break the cycles of abuse?

CHAPTER 10

Finding Freedom, Peace and Love

What was meant to destroy you only makes you stronger!!! Think of all the decisions and experiences that got you to where you are today. If it wasn't for those experiences, you would not be who you are today. Even your biggest mistakes can teach you something very important and valuable in your file. Think of those events and people as teachers propelling you to heal. Use that energy that once bogged down to propel you to live your dreams to the fullest. Find your strength in it and turn it around. You are strong for surviving, for being where you are today. Now you have the opportunity to live your best life.

Other victims did not make it. Many of them were killed or killed others. There are many in psychiatric wards and others on psychotic medicine. One of the first steps is to forgive yourself and the other person or people who harmed you. You may think, "How I can forgive someone who hurt me so much!" Trust me I understand your sentiment. This step is not for them, but for you. You do not have to let them know you forgave them, especially if you choose no contact. You can write a letter letting them know how they harmed you and forgive them. You do not have to send it. You can burn it or tear it up. I reiterate this is for you, not for them. You can also write a letter to yourself, forgiving and telling yourself how much you love you. You did the best you could under the circumstances and you were repeating your subconscious patterns. This knowledge was such a relief for me because I wasn't choosing it. It was something I had learned and I kept repeating. It was a living pattern ingrained in my brain since early childhood.

Peace

For me, in order to continue to find peace and love, I do the mirror work daily. Every morning is a new day and I build myself up before I hit the road or start working. I meditate, journal, read and spend time developing my peace. There are many situations and people I might face during the day that might affect me and bring me down. However, when I am grounded, I will not let those things or people affect me. When you see someone or something coming into your life trying to suck your energy, you will be able to cut them off and stop them in their tracks. This is how you will know you are at a new level. A different level where you will be able to find your peace, love and maintain it.

Freedom to Love

Finding the courage to be yourself and love yourself is liberating. Part of finding it is to continue to raise your vibrations. There is scientific evidence to demonstrate the heart is five thousand times more powerful than the brain. It is so important to love yourself,

God, your higher power and family. However, living from your heart is more powerful. What do I mean by living from the heart? Your heart is the most powerful organ in your body. It pumps two thousand gallons of blood per day. I will say it again, it pumps two tons of blood! That's amazing, and the energy it gives off is spectacular. It is more powerful than any other organ in your body. Everyone thinks the brain is the most powerful organ, but it is not. The heart's electrical field is about 60 times greater in amplitude than the electrical activity generated by the brain. When you start living from the heart, you're generating tremendous energy and sending it off into the universe. You will be happier living from your heart by doing the things you love and enjoy. Guess what the best part of all is? You will attract more love, peace and joy back to you by law of attraction. When two or more hearts are locked together, you can create a change in your neighborhood, city, state, country and the world. It starts with you and then it extends to those close to you. You impact everyone you come in contact with. I truly believe that love changes people who are open to it. Love is everything. Everyone yearns to be loved and accepted just the way they are. Love and acceptance is all people want.

To ignite these movements, it starts by loving yourself. I believe in the butterfly effect in what you do today will impact your future and those around you. It begins in your mind by your thoughts. You also want to keep in mind that perceptions are reality. Your perceptions lead to beliefs and those thoughts create actions. You can control your perception and how you see your world. If you don't believe in yourself, then you won't do it. Believe in yourself more than anyone else. Do not listen to the naysayers. You actually can achieve anything you set your mind to do. No matter how hard or difficult it is, you can do it if you believe in yourself. Visualization is key. Your thoughts create the energy you send off into your future. Your thoughts turn into energy in your body, which then puts your thoughts into motion to become a reality. You want to start seeing yourself happy. See yourself achieving success, whatever it means for you. See yourself successful into the future and doing the things you love. See yourself surrounded by people who love you. My first vision board included me laughing, living and enjoying life. I envisioned being my real authentic self, loving myself where I was and how I was. I wasn't trying to change anything about me. Have you done your vision board? If not, do one ASAP. You just need a board, images to paste and glue. Be sure to update your vision board once you create one. Hold your vision in your heart and mind every morning and every opportunity you get. Embrace it, believe it, breathe it and feel it throughout your body. Act as if you already have it. Start thanking God or your higher power for having what you dream for. IT IS YOURS!!!

Boundaries

In order to keep your peace, freedom and love, create boundaries. What are boundaries? I had no idea what they were before my healing process. Personal boundaries are guidelines, rules, or limits a person sets to identify reasonable, safe, and permissible ways for other people to behave towards you. They also state how someone will respond when someone passes those boundaries. Placing boundaries around you to say, "No, I will not allow this in my life" is perfectly acceptable to keep you safe. Do not allow anyone to make you feel bad or down about yourself or your situation. Speaking your truth and your feelings is important.

Since I never knew what boundaries were, I didn't have any boundaries much less enforced them. I was taught to obey my elders, the law, supervisor, husband and spiritual leaders. I was not taught that if something didn't feel right, I could say no. I wasn't taught to have my own opinion or express it. I was told to sit and be quiet, to only speak when spoken to. I now know I do have the right to think and speak my truth. I can choose who I want to have a relationship with and who not to. If people do not make me feel good, I do not need to put up with them. I definitely do not need to maintain a relationship with them. It was a realization that was very difficult for me to understand and wrap my brain around. However, this was so relieving to me when I did. We have the power to not accept toxicity in our lives.

If you find yourself stuck with a toxic person at work, you can request to be moved or speak to your manager about the situation. Try to find a solution so that you don't have to put up with it. Most companies want to provide a harassment free environment and it doesn't always have to be sexual. If they don't support you, then you have options. You have a choice not to accept it. Never accept people, places or things that do not bring you peace, love and joy.

In order to maintain your peace, continue your breathing and relaxation techniques we reviewed earlier. Write down your favorite techniques and take them with you wherever you go. You might need them at any given point during the day. Always remember you have tools in your pocket or purse to use when you need them. I usually do my breathing techniques when I'm driving or whenever I start feeling anxious. I listen to Hertz 432 sounds when working or when experiencing a stressful situation. You can practice prayer, meditation, or yoga at any time. Read books and affirmations that bring you peace. Journal your feelings, take bubble baths, take care of yourself, body, mind and soul. Remain in nature for at least 20 minutes every day in order to bring calmness and peace into your day.

The goal is to reduce living in a state of stress and anxiety to build up your mental health, prevent illnesses and keep your peace. You want to release all of the stress you accumulate every day. When you start your morning, focus on being your most natural powerful self, full of love and light. Keep raising your vibrations through breath work, food and other methods discussed in chapter 7. Nourish your body with natural organic food that won't harm your body.

There are so many toxins in packaged foods. Shampoos, toothpaste, deodorant, facial creams and make-up carry toxins. Do some research on the internet or instagram on the labels and learn how the ingredients affect your body. Example, research how aluminum found in deodorant affects women. Our diet and what we put on our skin affects us in so many ways. We are a product of what we eat, think and act on. If we feed ourselves good nutritious food, we will feel better over a longer period of time. Our thoughts are just as important. If we focus on all the bad things in our lives, we will attract more bad things. If we think only good things, we will attract more good things. When we don't take care of ourselves it shows up physically and emotionally. What do you want to attract into your life?

Taking care of ourselves includes having fun. A lot of people say, "I don't have time." Like with everything else, we should make time by scheduling it in the calendar and sticking to the plan. It's important to your mental health to go outside and exercise. You can go on a hike. You can take a trip. If you can make it to the ocean or a lake, the high vibrations will lift your spirit. Other ideas mentioned before: play games, listen to music, journal, ride a bike, paint, dance, etc. I love to take naps outside in a hammock between the trees, while listening to the wind through the leaves. It's just one of the most peaceful things I can do. When you're living in peace and find the freedom to do the things you love, you will find happiness. No one should ever stop you from achieving your goals and dreams.

Once you do, you will THRIVE! You will start to enjoy life and you will start to radiate and see the world differently than you did before.

It wasn't until I found quantum freedom healing when everything turned around and I was able to release and heal the toxic pain I had carried in my heart all these years. I was finally able to release the pain by facing it and self-partnering. I had to hold myself and love myself through the pain. I no longer ran away from it. I faced my worst fears from childhood. I learned the pattern I kept repeating over and over, stemming from my little baby girl who knew not how to cope with anything that happened to her. I saw how the trauma trapped in my subconscious mind kept repeating itself over and over again in my life. I was finally able to break the cycle of abuse in my life. I was finally able to laugh and enjoy life. I was able to find freedom and be myself. I'm no longer scared. I am living my best life. I am living my passions and dreams. I'm thankful to God and to all the people that helped make this a reality.

Today, I live from my heart and I keep my boundaries to protect myself from any toxicity or what does not make me happy. I have attracted people like me into my life and surround myself with like minded people. This process has truly made a difference for me. I was able to leave my corporate job of twenty three years. Now, I am able to start a new life doing the things that I love, like writing this book and focusing on the things and passions that make me happy. I love helping people and I want to help people break free from the cycles of abuse. I feel this is my mission and purpose in life. I absolutely love it. I feel free to do anything I want and I don't limit myself. I don't put a limit on what I can achieve. I do the things I love to the best of my ability every single day. Life has never been the same for me. I want the same for others who want to find freedom from abuse and live their dreams to the fullest.

CHAPTER 11

Living Your Best Life

You have come a long way. I salute you for making it this far. This is where you make quantum leaps in your life. You are the designer and creator of your life. Your thoughts and feelings create your life whether positive or negative. Your life is a manifestation of your thoughts. "Whatever the mind of man can conceive, it can achieve," a quote from W. Element Stone. You have the power to create your future with your thoughts and your will. The creative process has three steps. The first step: you must ask for what you want. I suggest you dream big and include details. How does living your best life look like? What are you doing in your best life? What are your surroundings? What does happiness look like? Close your eyes, image it, paint the picture. What does it **feel** like? Notice who, what, when, and where is around you in your happy place. Do not place limits. Think about, what would your perfect life look like? What motivates you? What are passions in your life? Create the world around you and write down what it looks like. What makes you happy? What gives you peace and joy? Think really big, do not limit yourself. I have dreamt big and obtained pretty much all the things I envisioned. I have traveled the world and enjoyed all the good things life has to offer. The things you love to do and are good at, are usually your purpose. The second step is to believe your desire or goal will become a reality. Once again your life is a manifestation of your thoughts. Affirm your goal and be grateful for it as if you already achieved it. Do not entertain worry or doubt, cement it in your brain. The third step is to receive it in your subconscious mind and make an emotional connection with it. It may take a while for your dream to manifest but in the meantime you can start to accept it and act as if you already have it. Become emotionally engaged with your dream. Invoke the feelings of gratitude for achieving the goal as if you already achieved it with an affirmation like this, "I am so happy and grateful now that I ...."

Bringing The Change

According to Dr. Lara Boyd, brain researcher at the University of British Columbia. Our brains change constantly and the old belief that our brain is set by the age of 8 is no longer true. Our brain is active even when we are resting. Every time we learn a new fact or skill, a change takes place in our brain. A concept called neuroplasticity. Recent study shows our brain is still rearranging as adults. It further shows how our behavior changes our brain. Age is not a factor in brain reorganization. Our brain re-org helps in recovery after a damage to your brain. The change occurs through the neurons and chemical concentrations in the cells. The structure of our brain changes to accommodate a new motor skill. However, it is stored in our short term memory. To maintain the changes, we have to keep practicing our new skill to log it into long term memory. When learning is taking place, the brain can alter its function. When you use a certain region it becomes more excited and easier to use again. The brain changes when and how it is activated. Neuroplasticity changes are supported by chemical, structural and functional changes across the whole brain in concert. They support learning taking place all the time. The biggest driver of change is our behavior. The problem why people don't learn as easily is due to the large amount of behavioral change or practice that must take place to learn and relearn new skills. Everyone has varying degrees of neuroplasticity. Nothing helps maintain the new changes than practice. Bottom line is you have to do the work. The more you struggle to learn the new skill, the more learning and structural changes that occur in the brain. On the flip side, your brain can also go down the negative side. You can easily forget, fall into addiction or have chronic pain. Everything we do affects changes in our brain. Everyone learns in a different way. Study how and what you learn best. Keep those behaviors that are healthy for your brain and break those behaviors that are not. Learning is about doing the work your brain requires. Some things may come more easily than others. Know that everything we do, encounter and experience has a potential to change our thinking and our brain for better or for worse. You have the power to build the brain and life you want. Once you dream your vision, hold on to it and write it down. To maintain the vision, practice seeing it daily, more than once a day, preferably in theta state. See how it feels and be grateful now for what you will have in the future. Many believe it takes 21 days to make a habit, but in reality it takes 66 days. If you visualize your dream daily, it will eventually become ingrained into your subconscious and you won't have to remember to think about it. It will become part of who you are and become a reality.

Belief in Your Vision

As Bob Proctor says, the moment you believe in something you fuse with the idea. If you can see it in your mind, you can hold it in your hand. If you don't believe it, you let it go. People let go of their goals and dreams because they do not know how to get there. If you hold your belief then you activate the sequence of its plots, plans, conditions and circumstances to see it come to reality. You rise to a new level and start to see the world through a different lense. This is the time when you start to act as if you are already there. See yourself living your dream whatever that might be. There is so much power in YOUR VISION. To illustrate how powerful this is, Dr. Waitley PH.D., asked his olympic athletes to visualize the race by closing their eyes and seeing the whole course. They were to see the whole race from beginning to end and see themselves at their peak performance in their mind. At the same time, he measured their brain waves and the same parts of the brain lit up as if they were actually running the race!!! The mind can not tell what is real or not, if you hold it in your mind, you can hold it in your hand.

You can create a new way of living. You will reach a new level that you can not feel with your five senses. Get away from only believing in what you can taste, touch or hear. Steve Jobs said, "You can't connect the dots looking forward, you can only connect them looking backwards. So you have to trust that the dots will somehow connect in the future." Imagine if he didn't hold on to his vision for the iPhone or other Apple products. How different would our world be? The Wright brothers had a vision of a plane in the air. They didn't know how they were going to do it, but they didn't give up until they accomplished it. You can not listen to the naysayers. If the Wright brothers had listened to the people who told them they were crazy, they would not have invented the first plane. You have to know with certainty that you can go anywhere you want to go. We all have what it takes to see our goals and dreams become a reality. Once you trigger your dream, you will attract the right people, places and things to come into your life to help you get to where you want to go. I know this happened to me! You are a co-creator of your life. Whatever you are thinking and feeling today is creating your future. You don't have to be a passenger and let opportunities pass you by. You do not have to watch your dreams in life skip over you. Visualize them and take action when the doors open up for you. Make decisions quickly based on faith, not on your current circumstances. Allow the energy to flow to you and through you without entertaining doubt or worry.

In order to move to a higher frequency, first accept and decide where you want to go. Once you visualize it, adapt to the new ideas and frequency it represents. It is not enough to just read it, you actually have to act as if you are operating from that level. According to Neville Goddard, "The future must become the present in the imagination of the one who consciously creates circumstance. We must translate vision into being a reality. Imagination must center itself upon some state and then view the world from that state." To move to a higher frequency, make the decision and see yourself in the future as if you are there now. Be thankful and grateful for the gift. As Mr. Proctor says, "We are only limited by weakness of attention and poverty of imagination. Earn more money, enjoy more freedom and begin to live the life you were designed to live." Adapt to the new ideas and feelings. Originate your wants and desires with your thoughts. Then the universe will come into play and you will attract more of the same until it becomes reality. In the beginning, you are operating from intuition and not from your five senses because it hasn't manifested yet. Be ready when you try to change to a new frequency, your old paradigm will resist the change and all hell will break loose. You must take conscious control over the old paradigm, remove it and replace it with your new paradigm. You can not let your old patterns take control. It feels like a person inside of you is fighting you, it's your old program telling you why you can't do it. "You don't have the money. You don't know how. You are never going to get anyone to believe in this." All of these thoughts are going to flood your brain. You have to fight them and take control over these negative thoughts. You have to implant and embed your new beliefs into your subconscious mind.

Ask yourself, what do I really want? Take a few minutes and write out your goals and dreams. Albert Einstein said, "The intuitive mind is a sacred gift and the rational mind is a faithful servant. We have created a society that honors the servant and has forgotten the gift." Let your mind take you where you want to go and be very specific. Think about how it feels to live and operate from there. When you start seeing yourself at the new level, think about the strategies you will use to combat your negative thoughts and naysayers in your life. How will you keep your will to continue to strive toward your goals? We all have doubts and we start to question if we can ever do this or not. Break through the terror barrier in order to achieve your goals and dreams. If your goal is big enough, the problems are going to be just as big but you have to keep moving forward. When you make a commitment, do it regardless of the circumstances, even if you do not have the resources. The problems will strengthen you. This is how I felt when I was walking through my snow storm. I could not see a foot in front of me, but I knew somehow, someway I would make it out. You have to hold on to your dreams and beliefs no matter what you go through. Remove the self-limiting belief that blocks you from living your best life. Once you do, you will be able to achieve the happiness you strive for in life. You will go from just surviving to thriving. This works in all aspects of life: health, wealth and relationships.

You are now living in your power, speaking your truth and being your authentic self. You are living from your heart. Trust your higher power and know you are supported. Truly love who you are and what you bring to the table. These true beliefs are where you want to live your life from. Start to believe in yourself and bring your focus into reality. Stay focused on the bigger picture, your vision and know the sky's the limit. If you think you can do it, then believe you will. Start by creating a plan and goals around your passions without any limitations. Don't think about limits on money or resources. Think about your abilities and desires. If you love it and it feels right to you then go for it. The ability is already inside of you. You already have the gift to make it reality, you don't need anything else. Start by taking action. Put your dreams into pictures and words on your vision board. Transferring your thoughts on paper makes it real and makes it come to fruition. It is simple and amazing how a little vision board will help your dreams come to life. When you create it, you're co-creating your future. No one else has the power to do it but you. You have the power to create the life that you want to live, but you have to believe it and take action. It sounds too good and easy to be true. However, believe in yourself and your dreams. A lot of people limit themselves and don't achieve the goals they want because they don't believe they can. Challenge yourself to change your paradigm, subconscious patterns and limiting beliefs about yourself. My first vision board came to reality and I am living my best life right now! I can not tell you how excited I am to be living my dreams!

Your life will continue to build upon your first level of achievement. Once you start increasing your beliefs and frequency you think from, more of the same will continue to appear in your life. Everything in this world vibrates at a certain frequency. You have to tune into that frequency much like we tune into AM or FM radio. Your phone vibrates at a certain frequency. Your dreams are found at a certain frequency. Increase your thoughts to those higher levels of frequency than where you are today. Surround yourself with like minded people. You will start to see these changes coming into reality in your life sooner than later. The law of attraction will come into play because it is the law of the universe. Do not limit yourself, that is the most important key here, don't limit, stop or block yourself from achieving success. Replace your old paradigms.

The law of inspired vision by Dr. Al Lundeen says if you stay within your truth, purpose and do what you love, your life will light up and you will reach your highest levels of achievement. You will excite your glial cells in your association cortex, just like Mr. Einstein's brain did and unleash your genius, see www.riseupradio.net Einstein's brain was kept hidden in a jar for almost 30 years until it was finally re-discovered by scientists. When they started doing analysis on his brain, they thought he would have more neurons or a larger size brain than most. In reality, his brain was very similar to other brains. The only significant difference was the large number of glial cells found in his left lower parietal lobe where higher mathematics and language abilities stem from. Prior to this discovery, scientists thought glial cells were like the glue that kept the brain together. However, we know Einstein worked on the things he loved. He was passionate about his work and became a genius as a result (Perry 2010) Link.

When we start working with our passions and doing the things we love, we start to increase our frequency to the highest levels. Remember when I asked if you did what you loved, it wouldn't be work? If you love it, you will enjoy it, and it won't feel like work. Work sounds like you are stuck doing something you don't love. Exchanging your hours for dollars and living paycheck to paycheck will not allow you the freedom you want and deserve. You want to spend your life doing the things you love and the money will naturally flow to you when you unlock your genius. Success will be yours because it is your passion and you will do exceedingly well doing what you love. The money will come from you doing your best work. When work becomes a grind, it energetically takes away from you because you're not enjoying what you do. Many of us do the jobs and take careers we're told to do from society, parents or caregivers. We don't do the things we love. I wanted to be an actress, singer, and dancer. I never followed those dreams or passions from childhood because I was told those were dead end dream jobs with no future. Clearly there are many actors, singers and dancers making a living doing what they love. I have since changed my dreams, although I still love singing. I love helping people grow and achieve their goals. Throughout all of the different jobs I had, coaching was my favorite and most rewarding. I helped many team members achieve success and move up in the company accomplishing their career goals. I am now coaching for a living and I love what I do. I have partnered with the best mentor ever, Bob Proctor to help people achieve their goals and dreams in life. It makes a world of difference when you do the things you love because you're living from the heart. You can find me at www.selenelifecoach.thinkingintoresults.com. As your heart gives more love into everything around you, you bring more positivity into your world and the people you work with. You become a magnet for people that share your passion, vision and dreams. You will be surrounded with people who help your vision become reality. Your vision continues to grow and reach more people.

Be real and true to yourself about the things you love and want to do in life. Do not focus on what other people say or what people do. The people you think were going to be your biggest supporters may not want to be. Your friends and/or family members may not share your new beliefs and that's ok. Do not let anyone or anything limit you or your potential. This is the reason it's so important to surround yourself with like minded people. Find people who will support you to live your dreams and passions with you. I have dedicated my whole life to help people achieve their dreams. This is when you start living your best life, being who you really are and enjoying the things you want to do. This is the best feeling ever.

I had to re-discover and uncover what makes me happy. I have a vision for my life and I'm not letting anyone stop me. No one can define happiness for me but me. I am doing what I love. I enjoy helping other people reach their goals and dreams. Everyone has passions. A very wise man, Benito Almanza, said to me, "Do what you love. Don't follow the money, it will naturally come to you for doing what you love." If you do what you love, your life will light up and others will see your light.

You will thrive and you will live your dreams. Remember, no one can make you happy but you. Breaking the cycles of abuse by self-partnering and not running away will allow divine healing into your heart, by being present with your pain and then releasing it. You can finally start healing those inner wounds and traumas. You don't have to survive your abuse. You can thrive as I have and thousands of other people all over the world. Be you, do not be afraid of who you are or your light. Let your light shine bright! Be a beacon of light and be the real authentic you.

References

Bell, L 2014, *What Happens to Your Body When You're Dreaming,* Women's Health, Hearst Digital Media, viewed 7 June 2020, <www.womenshealthmag.com/health/a19954389/dreaming/>

Epigenetics: Child development and Genes 2019, First Five Years, Goodstart Early Learning, viewed 7 June 2020, <https://www.firstfiveyears.org.au/child-development/epigenetics-child-development-and-genes>

Griffith's Et Al. n.d., *Where do gambling and internet 'addictions' belong?,* Nottingham, UK, viewed 7 June 2020, <*http://irep.ntu.ac.uk/id/eprint/29051/1/6552__Pontes.pdf*>

Haynes 2020, *Ike and Tina Turner's Tumultuous Relationship,* Biography, A&E Television Networks, viewed 7 June 2020, <www.biography.com/.amp/news/tina-turner-ike-relationship>

Medical News Today 2020, *What are genes and why are they important?*, Healthline Media, viewed 7 June 2020, <https://www.medicalnewstoday.com/articles/120574#what_are_they_made_of>

Mental Health America 2020, *Co-Dependency,* Better Help, viewed 7 June 2020, Alexandria, VA, <https://www.mhanational.org/issues/co-dependency>

National Association of Adult Survivors of Child Abuse 2011, *What are the statistics of the abused?*, LACP org, viewed 7 June 2020, <http://www.naasca.org/2012-Resources/010812-StaisticsOfChildAbuse.htm>

Reynolds 2019, *Having Empathy and Being an Empath: What's the Difference?*, Psychology Today, Sussex Publishers, viewed 7 June 2020 <*www.psychologytoday.com/us/blog/human-kind/201901/having-empathy-and-being-empath-what-s-the-difference*>

Perry 2010, *Glia: the Other Brain Cells,* Brain Facts, Society for Nueroscience, viewed 7 June 2020, <https://www.brainfacts.org/archives/2010/glia-the-other-brain-cells>

Shiel W 2017, *Medical Definition of Post-traumatic Stress Disorder*, Medicine Net, viewed 7 June 2020 <www.medicinenet.com/script/main/art.asp?articlekey=18779>

Scitable 2014, *Cell Signaling*, Nature Education, viewed 7 June 2020, <https://www.nature.com/scitable/topicpage/cell-signaling-14047077/>

The Tapping Solution 2020, *What is Tapping and How Can I Start Using It?*, viewed 7 June 2020,

<https://www.thetappingsolution.com/tapping-101/>

The Cycles of Abuse n.d., Manitoba Government, viewed 7 June 2020, <https://www.gov.mb.ca/msw/fvpp/cycle.html>

Wilkinson 2017, *What is Gaslighting? The 1944 film Gaslight is the Best Explainer,* Vox Media, viewed 7 June 2020, <www.vox.com/platform/amp/culture/2017/1/21/14315372/what-is-gaslighting-gaslight-movie-ingrid-bergman>

WHAT DO YOU REALLY WANT???

Reach Your Dreams with Me at Link: SeleneChangeYourLiife

Shop with me at Link: SeleneShopify *-50% of proceeds go to help abuse victims*

Let's Get Social

Selene Life Coach https://bit.ly/SeleneYouTube

Instagram https://bit.ly/SeleneLifeCoach

Selene Life Coach https://bit.ly/SeleneFBgroup

Selene Hernandez https://bit.ly/SeleneLinkedIn

Selene Life Coach https://bit.ly/SeleneTikTok

Selene Life Coach https://bit.ly/SeleneTwitter

Let's Continue the Conversation
#SeleneLifeCoach
Email: selene@selenelifecoach.com

THANK YOU FOR READING MY BOOK!

FREE BONUS GIFT

Just to say thanks for buying and reading my book, I would like to give you a free bonus gift that will add value and that you will appreciate, 100% FREE, no strings attached!

To Download Now, Visit:

http://www.SeleneLifeCoach.com/SB/freegift

I appreciate your interest in my book and I value your feedback as it helps me improve future versions of this book. I would appreciate it if you could leave your invaluable review on Amazon.com with your feedback. Thank you!

Made in the USA
Monee, IL
05 December 2020